"Those who have admired and been formed over the years by Lewis Smedes's faith-filled and thought-provoking writing will rejoice in this new gathering of his work. Thanks to Crosby's deft hand as editor and compiler, there's now a small bit of Smedes-at-his-best for every day of the working week over an entire year."

PHYLLIS TICKLE, compiler of *The Divine Hours*

"Lew Smedes was known for his grace and his authenticity. These fragments of his writings will make you take stock of your true self and learn to love it as God does. Faithfully chew on these bits over a year's time, and you will grow in faith, hope and love."

DAVID NEFF, editor and vice president, *Christianity Today*

"Lewis Smedes offered a prophetic voice of grace in a world where we struggle to grasp such a thing. *Days of Grace Through the Year* allows Smedes's words to keep reverberating in our daily lives, helping us remember the most radical truth claim of Christianity—that the Eternal Word became human and dwelled among us, full of grace and truth."

MARK R. McMINN, author of *Sin and Grace in Christian Counseling*

"Really good writing and thinking seem to be in short supply these days, but wisdom is an even rarer commodity. In *Days of Grace Through the Year*, Jeff Crosby has gathered a wonderful collection of excerpts from the pen of one of the twentieth century's wisest writers, Lewis Smedes. Page after page is filled with practical, discerning and mature insight on how to live with greater authenticity, passion and emotional health. This is a book that deserves to be carefully pondered and acted upon."

TERRY GLASPEY, author of *Not a Tame Lion: The Spiritual Legacy of C. S. Lewis and the Chronicles of Narnia*

"These reflections are snippets from a man of great soul. They are alternately buckets of ice water, floating feathers, branding irons, gentle winds, flame throwers, unblinking stares and more. I eagerly read them in hope, stirred up by honest faith, and challenged to live more attentively toward God and one another each day."

MARK LABBERTON, author of *The Dangerous Act of Worship*

DAYS OF GRACE

Through the Year

Lewis B. Smedes

Compiled and edited by Jeff Crosby

IVP Books

An imprint of InterVarsity Press
Downers Grove, Illinois

InterVarsity Press
P.O. Box 1400, Downers Grove, IL 60515-1426
World Wide Web: www.ivpress.com
E-mail: email@ivpress.com

InterVarsity Press® is the book-publishing division of InterVarsity Christian Fellowship/USA®, a student movement active on campus at hundreds of universities, colleges and schools of nursing in the United States of America, and a member movement of the International Fellowship of Evangelical Students. For information about local and regional activities, write Public Relations Dept., InterVarsity Christian Fellowship/USA, 6400 Schroeder Rd., P.O. Box 7895, Madison, WI 53707-7895, or visit the IVCF website at <www.intervarsity.org>.

All Scripture quotations, unless otherwise indicated, are taken from the Holy Bible, New International Version®. NIV®. Copyright ©1973, 1978, 1984 by International Bible Society. Used by permission of Zondervan Publishing House. All rights reserved.

The writings of Lewis B. Smedes have been adapted for use in this volume. For a list of rightsholders for previously published material, please turn to pages 321-22.

Design: Cindy Kiple

Images: John Lawrence/Getty Images

ISBN 978-0-8308-3296-5

Printed in the United States of America ∞

Library of Congress Cataloging-in-Publication Data

Smedes, Lewis B.
  Days of grace through the year/Lewis B. Smedes; compiled and
edited by Jeff Crosby
    p. cm.—(Through the year devotionals)
  ISBN 978-0-8308-3296-5 (pbk.: alk. paper)
  1. Devotional literature. I. Crosby, Jeff (Jeff J.) II. Title.
  BV4811.S64 2007
  242'.2—dc22

                         2007016616

P	20	19	18	17	16	15	14	13	12	11	10	9	8	7	6	5	4	3	2	1
Y	24	23	22	21	20	19	18	17	16	15	14	13	12	11	10	09	08	07

I can't remember exactly when or where I first read something by Lew Smedes, but I remember my reaction. I was in my teens, judgmental in the way that kids can be when they listen to their elders, and so many of the Christian voices I heard—whether in person or via the radio or on the printed page—repelled me. I didn't want to be associated with an enterprise that routinely produced such unctuous talk. (My own sense of superiority went unexamined.) Smedes was different, and once I'd learned his name I kept an eye out for it.

Different how, exactly? He was blunt, direct. He spoke in the voice that men and women use when they talk about their jobs and their families and all the stuff of everyday life, sex included, but he was talking about matters such as shame and forgiveness and grace (and sex).

You can sense that difference in the selections included in this devotional reader. You'll notice Smedes' preference for short sentences and pithy statements: "Some people believe that you should not forgive anyone who wronged you unless he or she crawls back on his knees, says he or she is sorry, and begs you to forgive him. I think that is a bad idea." Or how about this: "Realism is the secret of love's patience. Love is not idealism; it does not have to be fanatic. It is not hysterical; it knows the world is not going to fall apart unless we immediately clean up every mess." That's wisdom won in marriage, a school where we can learn so much, if we are willing.

Like most writers, Smedes had different voices for different occasions. He could be wickedly funny. That's a side of him not much represented in this admirable collection, but it's important to remember as you read. To give you an idea of what I have in mind, let me quote from "Evangelicalism—A Fantasy," a brilliant little piece originally published in *The Reformed Journal* in 1980. In it, Smedes imagines an "evangelical College of Cardinals" convened at a Holiday Inn in Wheaton, Illinois

to discuss, in alphabetical order, this year's doubtful leaders. The discussion is somber, frank, and manifestly painful for everyone. Finally, as things must, it comes to a vote. Each ballot has one name at the top, and two squares—one labeled "Tolerated," the other "Not Tolerated." The ballots are collected and counted, and only the names of the nontolerated are announced. The secretary first declares—with a trace of unction—"non est tolerandus," and then gives the name of the fallen leader.

Their solemn work done, the cardinals bow for a "word of prayer," shake hands, wish each other God's blessing, pick up their briefcases, sign out, climb back into the shuttle bus to O'Hare, arriving in time to catch their flights back to their respective headquarters.

Bull's-eye. You'll be in good company as you follow Lew Smedes through the year.

John Wilson
Editor, Books & Culture

W elcome to the through-the-year devotionals. This small book offers you a wonderful opportunity to reflect each day on the grace and goodness of God, drawing you to him in worship, wonder, praise and thanksgiving.

The selections are drawn from the writings of Lewis B. Smedes, whose focus on the themes of grace, gratitude, forgiveness and the love of God have touched countless lives. In his spiritual memoir *My God and I*, Smedes's penchant for understatement shone through when he wrote that most of his books "have not been expressly about God but about human life and how it can and should be lived." Yet, in reflecting how life should be lived, his writings have ultimately pointed us back to God and the wonder of his grace through Jesus Christ.

In one of the meditations you'll find here, Smedes writes, "the flagship word of the gospel is *grace*. No wonder, for *grace* is shorthand for God wishing us well." This notion of God wishing us well is one of the key characteristics of Smedes's published works, and one of the themes you'll find running throughout *Days of Grace Through the Year*.

You'll find a year's worth of devotions here, designed to fill six days a week. We choose to offer six entries each week rather than seven, assuming that you'll use at least one day a week for worshiping God with his gathered people in your church—and also for a built-in day of grace, as circumstances do sometimes infringe on our devotional time. You might use the seventh day to go back to some of the suggestions at the end of the week's devotional entries. These devotions are not dated; you can start anywhere and move around as you please, but they are organized such that they are best read a week at a time.

Because reading without response has little effect, responding to what God has said to you in the daily meditation is important. At the end of each entry you'll find a suggested activity to aid in your response to the Scripture and that day's devotion. You may be invited to reflect, pray, meditate or journal. These suggestions are just a place to start, however, since meditation and prayer naturally intertwine—one leading to the other.

If the reflection raises confusion, you will find it helpful to write your thoughts on paper. Some prayers are likewise better written than spoken. A written prayer is just as worshipful as a prayer thought or spoken, and the process of writing gives you a chance to carefully phrase what you say to God—and then come back to it later.

◆ ◆ ◆

I'd like to extend my gratitude to Lewis Smedes's widow, Doris B. Smedes, for her encouragement and assistance on this project, both of which came at a critical juncture of the book's development. Special thanks are also due to my wife, Cindy Crosby, and to Ann Swindell for their contributions of time and support as the compilation drew to a close.

May you know the rich grace of God in fresh, new ways as you read through the year.

Jeff Crosby

MONDAY

A Family Reunion

We had to celebrate and rejoice,
because this brother of yours was dead and has come to life;
he was lost and has been found.

LUKE 15:32 NRSV

Jesus once told a beautiful story about how a Hebrew father welcomed his son back home after the son had done him wrong. It is such a favorite Bible story, I suppose, because it tells us that our heavenly Father takes us back after we have done him wrong the way the father in the story took his son back. The story has been retold thousands of times as a story of forgiveness. Actually, it is about a family reunion.

God invites all the thirsty, the hungry, and the prodigals whom he forgives back to their true home: "You shall go out in joy, and be led back in peace; the mountains and hills before you shall burst into song" (Isaiah 55:12 NRSV). The flagship word of the gospel is *grace*. No wonder, for *grace* is shorthand for God wishing us well.

PRAY: *Offer a prayer of thanksgiving for God's welcoming you into his family.*

The Power to Love

Who is wise and understanding among you?
Show by your good life that your works are done with gentleness born of wisdom.

JAMES 3:13 NRSV

A person of discernment can be wrong sometimes, is hardly ever totally right. And we are all better off when we have enough discernment to know that we could at any moment be quite mistaken, all wrong—or only half right—about what we think we see.

We are not zapped with imaginative discernment. We get it by working at our native skills and by keeping our hearts open to love. It takes practice, and it never comes with a certainty that no one can contradict.

JOURNAL: *In what areas of your life do you need to discern God's leading and direction? Write these areas down and pray for moments of grace.*

For God alone my soul waits in silence. . . .
He alone is my rock and my salvation, my fortress; I shall not be shaken.

PSALM 62:5-6 NRSV

As I have grown old, my feelings about God have tapered down to gratitude and hope.

Gratitude is the pleasure of hope come true. Hope is the pain of gratitude postponed. Gratitude comes easy, on its own steam, whenever we know that someone has given us a real gift. Hope comes harder, sometimes with our backs against the wall, laden with doubts that what we hope for will ever come. Gratitude always feels good, as close to joy as any feeling can get. Hope can feel unbearable; when we passionately long for what we do not have and it is taking too long to come, we are restless as a farmer waiting for rain after an August without a drop.

REFLECT: *For what do you feel gratitude today? For what are you still waiting in hope?*

A Generous Joy

> They lift up their voices, they sing for joy;
> they shout from the west over the majesty of the LORD.

ISAIAH 24:14 NRSV

Every silver lining has a cloud. Cloudless joy comes when everything is right, when cancer never strikes and swords have become plowshares, when all children dance safely in the streets, and all tears are wiped away. When Shalom comes, then joy will have no clouds. But between now and then, joy comes between the clouds.

If all must be right with the world before I may have a fling with joy, I shall be somber forever.

Joy in a world that does not work right must be a generous joy. Joy is always, always in spite of the fact that the whole world is groaning while it waits for its redemption.

REFLECT: *When have you felt a deep touch of joy between the clouds of life? What is clouding your experience of joy these days? What will it take for you to be generous in your practice of joy today?*

The Best of Intentions

Forgive them, for they do not know what they are doing.

LUKE 23:34

If only people with bad intentions did bad things to people, the world would be a safer place to live. It is the people who do bad things with good intentions that make the world a dangerous planet. The roads to our earthly hells are often paved with other people's good intentions.

After the black people of South Africa won the battle against apartheid, the white former prime minister, F. W. de Klerk, said: "Apartheid was a well-intentioned system that failed." Come now, can people really do such gigantic evil with good intentions? Of course they can. The better the intentions, the easier it is to do the harm.

It may just be that the very worst of harm is done by people with the best of intentions. "Forgive them," our Lord prayed, dying on the cross, "they do not know what they are doing." His killers had the best of intentions; they were only ridding Israel of a blasphemer. But they actually crucified the Lord with their good intentions.

APPLY: *Think back to a time when your good intentions had undesirable outcomes? Pray for and receive God's forgiveness for those moments.*

Annoyances

> A person's wisdom yields patience;
> it is to one's glory to overlook an offense.

PROVERBS 19:11 TNIV

Our lives are sprinkled with annoyances. I can't stand the kind of shoppers who check out fifteen items in the eight-item express lane and then talk about their cat with their cashier, while I wait impatiently to pay for one carton of milk. I drive my wife crazy by switching channels mindlessly on the television set. She annoys me when she stretches short stories she tells at dinner into full-length novels. These are nettles against our tender skin; but they are probably not deep enough to raise the issue of forgiveness.

If we were to turn every nuisance into a crisis of forgiveness, our conversations would become revolving reconciliations. Better to swallow annoyances and leave forgiveness for the deeper hurts.

REFLECT: *What annoys you? How can Christ help you swallow these annoyances?*

M O N D A Y *Spiritual Surgery*

> *When you stand praying, if you hold anything against anyone,*
> *forgive him, so that your Father in heaven may forgive you your sins.*

MARK 11:25

When you forgive someone for hurting you, you perform spiritual surgery inside your soul; you cut away the wrong that was done to you so that you can see your "enemy" through the magic eyes that can heal your soul. Detach that person from the hurt and let it go, the way a child opens his hands and lets a trapped butterfly go free.

Then, invite that person back into your mind, fresh, as if a piece of history between you had been rewritten, its grip on your memory broken. Reverse the seemingly irreversible flow of pain within you.

As we forgive people, we gradually come to see the deeper truth about them, a truth our hate blinds us to, a truth we can see only when we separate them from what they did to us.

PRAY: *Take time to pray for someone who has injured you. Ask God to show you a deeper truth about them.*

Truthfulness

> *Buy the truth and do not sell it; get wisdom, discipline and understanding.*
> PROVERBS 23:23

Truthfulness is a state of mind; it has to do with your real intentions. You must want your words to carry your real intentions. What you say must vibrate with what you feel in your heart. Harmony between the message you give to the outside world and the feelings you keep on the inside.

But there is one thing more about truthfulness, just one thing. You must at least try to bring both your heart and your words in tune with reality. This is the truthfulness those you forgive must bring with them as their entrée back into your life. To be specific, you must expect those who hurt you to be honestly in touch with the reality of your falling-out, your pain and their responsibility for them.

JOURNAL: *Where is there currently disharmony between the message you give to the outside world and your deep-seated feelings? Journal your thoughts about this.*

New Starts

> *What strength do I have, that I should still hope?*
> *What prospects, that I should be patient? Do I have the strength of stone? Is my flesh bronze?*
> *Do I have any power to help myself, now that success has been driven from me?*

JOB 6:11-13

We practice love's high art framed and fringed by the boundaries of time and place. We heal the wounds of our painful pasts, but the healing is limited by things that have happened to us during the time since our falling-out began. We make our new beginnings, not where we used to be or where we wish we could be, but only where we are and with what we have at hand.

Accepting limits is its own kind of honest. Wine out of water, OK—but, please, not out of Elmer's glue! New beginnings must fit within the arena of one's own circumstances. The only day we ever have to forgive each other in is *this* one, the day we have at hand; and with the options we have on this particular day we must make our new starts on the adventure of reconciliation.

REFLECT: *What "new beginnings" do you desire to make? Think of the options you have on this particular day, and make your start on the adventure.*

THURSDAY

The Birth of Hope

May your unfailing love rest upon us, O LORD,
even as we put our hope in you.

PSALM 33:22

Hope is born the moment we believe that the good things we wish for and imagine having are possible for us to have. The odds may be against us, but hope does not calculate the odds. All hope needs is a belief that what we hope for is possible.

Hope is so closely linked to faith that the two tend to blend into one. The Bible says that "faith (or trust) is the substance of things hoped for" (see Hebrews 11:1). This is true of faith in God, but it is also true of all other faith. No matter what we put our faith *in*, when faith goes, hope goes with it. In some ways, hope *is* faith—faith with its eyes on possibilities for the future.

APPLY: *What possibilities for the future do you hold in faith and hope?*

The Best Things in Life

Find rest, O my soul, in God alone; my hope comes from him.

PSALM 62:5

The whisper of a wish, like the cry of a newborn child, is the first sure sign that hope is being born—an early yearning, a late longing, sometimes a passion, but at least a desire. We only hope for what we wish for. Wish not, hope not.

Somewhere the poet T. S. Eliot quipped that the Maker of the universe exults in every newly fanned desire. God wants us to wish, I think, because when we have no more wishes to wish, our hope dies of premature contentment. And when I think about the best things in life that I have long wished for, I am encouraged by C. S. Lewis's remark that "our best havings are our wantings."

JOURNAL: *How vulnerable is your hope to death by "premature contentment"? Write down a list of "wishes to wish" somewhere you'll be easily able to revisit from time to time to assess what has become of your wishes.*

Seeing with Our Souls

Now we see but a poor reflection as in a mirror; then we shall see face to face.
Now I know in part; then I shall know fully, even as I am fully known.

1 CORINTHIANS 13:12

To see *beyond* what is to what can be. Or to see *within* what seems to be to what *really* is. This is imagination. There can be no hope without it.

We may see it fantastically, as dreamers in restless nights see sublime and hideous things beyond the horizon of sense. We may see it through a gauze dimly or a glass darkly, as an old man sees the world through cataracts. But if we see it at all, and if we wish for what we see, we are on the verge of hoping for it.

The link between imagination and hope is broken if we think that imagination is *only* for such things as fables, fantasies and fairly tales. We do imagine things that are not real, thank God; what should we do without fairy stories and happy endings? But imagining things is also a way of seeing the most real things of all, things for which we need lenses in our souls as well as in our heads.

JOURNAL: *What is the relationship, in your life, between your imagination and your ability to hope? Take time to journal your thoughts and feelings.*

M O N D A Y

The Raw Materials of Hope

Those who hope in the LORD will renew their strength. They will soar on wings like eagles;
they will run and not grow weary, they will walk and not be faint.

ISAIAH 40:31

I believe that one day life will win over death, that good will win over evil, that love will win over hate, that joy will win over sadness, and that the whole world will work the way its Creator intended it to work. I want it desperately, I can imagine what it would be like, and I believe that with God it is possible. I have no hard evidence that such goodness is *likely* to heal our broken world. But I do have my reasons for believing it *can*. The reasons all compress into one: God. God is; therefore I hope. I hope; therefore I am.

These then—wishing, imagining and believing—are the stuff that hope is made of. Call them the raw materials of hope if you wish. The point is that hope begins to stir in me when I truly wish for things I do not have. It takes on a life of its own when I imagine what it would be like if my wish were granted. And hope arrives ripe and mature when I believe that the dream I want to come true *can* come true.

PRAY: *Reread the passage from Isaiah. Ask the Lord to renew your strength as you wait in hope for the things you wish were true in the world.*

Hope, the Child of Faith

Who of you by worrying can add a single hour to his life?

MATTHEW 6:27

Some people try to use faith as a wedge into the worry-free life. But faith does not put worry to sleep. Hope is the child of faith, and worry is the child of doubt. But doubt is the twin sister of faith. The French theologian Jacques Ellul had it just right: "The person who is plunged into doubt is not the unbeliever but the person who has no other hope but hope." Unbelievers do not have to doubt. Believers *doubt* precisely because they live by faith and not by sight. And they *hope* precisely because they live by faith. So worry tags along with doubt as long as we live by faith and hope.

One of the more hopeful ways of expressing faith is to say that, while we do not know what the future holds, we know who holds the future.

JOURNAL: *What difference does God's holding of the future make in the midst of our worry and doubt?*

Keep On Waiting

> *"For I know the plans I have for you," declares the LORD,*
> *"plans to prosper you and not to harm you, plans to give you hope and a future."*
>
> JEREMIAH 29:11

Nelson Mandela had to wait in prison for twenty-seven years before his hope of a new South Africa could be achieved. As the day of his freedom drew close, his only daughter was allowed to come and see him. When she came, she carried with her the grandchild Mandela had never seen. She had waited to name the child until her grandfather could give her a name. "I don't think a man was ever happier to hold a baby than I was that day," he wrote in his memoirs. Mandela named her Zaziwe, an African word for hope. He called her Hope, he said, because "during all my years in prison hope never left me—and now it never would."

What we often forget is that though worry is almost automatic, we have to make a decision, many decisions sometimes, to keep on waiting. People will tell us to give it up, to let hope die and let worry die with it. And they have us almost convinced. But we decide to keep on waiting. And our decision to keep waiting shapes the whole of our living.

PRAY: *Use the passage from Jeremiah 29 as a prayer of thanksgiving for your future days.*

The Power of Hope

But as for me, I watch in hope for the LORD,
I wait for God my Savior; my God will hear me.

MICAH 7:7

In his memorable book *Man's Search for Meaning*, Viktor Frankl helped us comprehend the waiting power of hope. He told us about Jews who kept waiting for the day they would get out of their concentration camps when any eye could see they would die there. They kept waiting because they kept hoping. But what earthly good did it do them to wait for what was so unlikely to happen?

Frankl's answer was that in waiting for escape those Jews were making a claim on their own sacred identity and the meaning and purpose of their lives. The guards drummed it into their heads every hour that they were pigs, vermin, scum of the earth. But as long as they remembered that they were the children of God, they kept on waiting. And as long as they waited, they maintained the dignity of the children of God.

REFLECT: *What do you see as your purpose in life? In what ways does that understanding affect how you wait for your hopes to be fulfilled?*

The Infectious Force of Hope

Be joyful in hope, patient in affliction, faithful in prayer.

ROMANS 12:12

People who have the habit of hope live better than people who have the habit of despair. They are ever so much happier. They respond more effectively to crises. They are stricken but not crushed by tragedy. When everything good about life shakes at the foundations and they cannot be sure of what will happen next, they turn their eyes to the possibility that something good can still come of it. And then they act on the possibilities of rescuing some good out of it all. They often do the hoping for their families, their children and their friends, and pull the others through the tough times by the infectious force of their hopes.

APPLY: *How can you cultivate the "habit of hope" in your daily life?*

God Is on Hope's Side

Faith is being sure of what we hope for and certain of what we do not see.

HEBREWS 11:1

I have learned a lot about how to counter inherited despair by setting my mind on a faith that better things are possible. It's a tug-of-war, I admit, and my heels are dug in for a long pull before hope has a firm and steady grip on my spirit. In the morning, despair may have the edge. By midday hope may surge back. But I believe that despair will not win the struggle for my soul. Hope will always fight back and in the end prevail because God is on hope's side.

I no longer believe that people who have the habit of hoping are tripped into hopefulness by a lucky destiny. I believe that, though their raw materials have made it easier for them, they too must choose to hope and to reject despair when they enter the time of trouble.

JOURNAL: *What does it mean to say "God is on hope's side"? What difference does it make in the life of the believer?*

M O N D A Y *Inventory of Hopes*

> The LORD delights in those who fear him,
> who put their hope in his unfailing love.

PSALM 147:11

We are not always sure whether the things we hope for are means of making still other hopes come true or whether they are what we want for their very own sakes. Why do you hope for a good education for your children? Or for more beauty in your life? Or for love and friendship? Or for getting closer to God? Are these means or ends? Nobody knows but you.

We need to know what we hope for because our hopes are too important to leave in a jumbled heap like a basket of unsorted laundry. We all tend to become what we most hope for, so taking inventory of our hopes is a way of taking inventory of our future selves.

One thing we know for sure: we have to do our *own* inventory. Nobody else can tell us what we really *do* hope for or *why* we hope for them. Others may tell us what we *ought* to hope for. But only we can know what we actually *do* hope for.

JOURNAL: *Take an inventory of your hopes for the future. Which are means? Which are ends?*

Hope That Mellows with Age

Guide me in your truth and teach me, for you are God my Savior,
and my hope is in you all day long.

PSALM 25:5

Make no mistake about it, our hopes do not become more spiritual just because we are getting closer to the time for discarding our bodies. And yet, I find that my hope mellows some with age; my early discontent with the way things were is melting down to gratitude for the way things are. I am sometimes stunned by how much better my life is than I once dared hope it would be. And I find myself (bit by bit) adjusting my earlier hopes that were born of discontent with the way things were to a more serene hope that I will be content at last with whatever God wills to give.

PRAY: *Using Psalm 25:5 as your starting point, ask God to guide you and teach you his truth as you put your hope in him.*

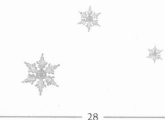

A Hope for Goodness

But as for me, I will always have hope; I will praise you more and more.

PSALM 71:14

A survivor of Auschwitz told me that every now and then he takes his grandchildren with him to revisit the site of the death camp. Why? To keep his hate alive? To make sure his grandchildren hate the people who did this to him? Not for either of these reasons. He goes back to show his grandchildren the miracle of his survival. To let his grandchildren know that men are capable of horrible evil. And to move them early on to hope that they will do great good instead.

We would not hope for goodness if we did not know evil. We would live in the illusion that the way things are is the way they are supposed to be. And we would feel no need to hope that they could ever get to be the way they are supposed to be.

REFLECT: *What evil in the world today is most distressing for you? How can you move from distress to hope in the face of this evil?*

Rekindling Our Hope

Praise be to the God and Father of our Lord Jesus Christ!
In his great mercy he has given us new birth into a living hope
through the resurrection of Jesus Christ from the dead.

1 PETER 1:3

Christians celebrate the death of Jesus in the Lord's Supper to remember that he died on the cross for the sins of the world. But the supper does not end with the recollection of suffering. We listen to the Lord telling his disciples to repeat this same memorial until he returns. Listening, we rekindle our hope that he will indeed return and that, when he does, God will make his world right again for everyone. That he will see to it that, once and for all, all will be well with the world and all will be well with all of his children.

REFLECT: *How would a spirit of hope rather than of remembrance affect your experience of communion?*

Counting Our Blessings

Praise be to the God and Father of our Lord Jesus Christ,
who has blessed us in the heavenly realms with
every spiritual blessing in Christ.

EPHESIANS 1 : 3

"Count your blessings," went an old gospel song that we sang a lot during the Great Depression, "name them one by one. Count your many blessings, see what God has done." For too long, I thought life was too tough to be tenderized by such simple blue-sky piety. Now I know by experience that counting the blessings I remember is the surest way to keep alive hope for blessings still to come.

I recall Benjamin Weir and how he kept his hope alive while he was a hostage in Lebanon and blessings came one by one, in small packages that were not always easy to spot. "How did you spend your time during all those months?" reporters asked him after he was released.

"Counting my blessings."

PRAY: *Write or say aloud a prayer of thanksgiving for blessings remembered and blessings to come.*

Being a Vicarious Hoper

For the sake of my brothers and friends, I will say, "Peace be within you."

PSALM 122:8

The best gift parents can give a dispirited and despairing child is to give him clear signals that *they* hope *for* him. The best thing a friend can do for a despairing friend is to be her vicarious hoper. The best therapy begins when a client who has lost hope in himself is convinced that his therapist has hope for him. The best church we can belong to is one that not only preaches hope for the world, but demonstrates to us that it has hope for us.

APPLY: *How can you, through your church or in your neighborhood, demonstrate hope for the people you come in contact with?*

MONDAY

A Way Paved by Forgiveness

If your brother sins, rebuke him, and if he repents, forgive him.
If he sins against you seven times in a day,
and seven times comes back to you and says, "I repent," forgive him.

LUKE 17:3-4

In a world like ours, where people hurt each other badly and wrong each other in the bargain, we can get ourselves stuck forever to a bad past that steals away our hope for a better future. The memory of how a trusted friend or spouse or parent violated our trust can so mesmerize our spirits that it locks our minds to the memory. And as long as we are hostage to the memory, we are not free to hope.

Life offers only one way to drain the hate and replace it with hope. Once wounded and wronged, our way back into hope for the future is the way out of the bilge of bitterness about the past—a way paved by forgiveness.

APPLY: *Are there memories from your past to which you feel held hostage? Whom do you need to consider forgiving in order to be free to hope?*

At the Edge of the Sea

If I take the wings of the morning, and dwell in the uttermost parts of the sea;
even there shall thy hand lead me, and thy right hand shall hold me.

PSALM 139:9-10 KJV

The uttermost parts of the sea, the edge of the sea—as far as the ancient psalmist knew—was literally the rim of the earth. Beyond the edge, where the sea stopped, there was only a bottomless abyss, endless *nothing*. If you took one step too far, you would trip into a black hole of infinite nothingness where you would be beyond the reach of God.

Being at the edge of the sea is a metaphor for the experience of losing control of your life. When you sense that the foundations are shaking and that at any moment the bottom is going to drop out of your life, and you have no one to reach down and pull you up, no one who can help you get your feet on the ground again; when not even God can stop your free fall into ruin; when, in short, you are a goner for sure, that is when you are at the edge of the sea.

But not to worry: if you should ever trip and fall out of God's presence, you will discover that he is there after all.

REFLECT: *Psalm 139 is a song of hope and comfort. Reread the passage above or, better, the entire psalm from your Bible and reflect on its metaphors as truth for your life today.*

> I press on toward the goal to win the prize
> for which God has called me heavenward in Christ Jesus.

PHILIPPIANS 3 : 14

Karl Barth, notoriously wordy otherwise, used just one word to tell us what it is that we have when we have salvation: it is *fulfillment*. "Salvation is fulfillment, the supreme sufficient, definitive, and indestructible fulfillment of (our) being." This, it seems to me, is what our hearts are most deeply restless for—our deepest desire, never totally experienced in this life—the total fulfillment of our very beings that is possible only in God. When we want this, heaven is what we want.

PRAY: *Share with God your sense of being unfulfilled today. Pray for God's salvation to be more fully realized in your life.*

Images of Heaven

> *In my Father's house are many rooms; if it were not so, I would have told you.*
> *I am going there to prepare a place for you.*

JOHN 14:2

Some of our truest images of ourselves in heaven are stirred up by bread-and-butter pleasures we enjoy here. Have a thigh-thumping laugh at a ridiculous story, and you get a sharp snap of yourself happy in heaven. Let a piece of soul music send shivers up your spine, and you have an image of your capacity for beauty in heaven. Watch a giggling two-year-old toddle into his mother's arms, and you get a fairly good image of yourself in heaven with God. Maybe the happiest memories of ourselves on earth are our clearest images of what we shall be in heaven.

REFLECT: *What images are conjured up in your mind when you think of heaven?*

A Frayed Fabric

Guard my life and rescue me; let me not be put to shame, for I take refuge in you.

PSALM 25:20

Shame is about our very *selves*—not about some bad thing we *did* or *said* but about what we *are*. It tells us that we *are* unworthy. Totally. It is not as if a few seams in the garment of ourselves need stitching; the whole fabric is frayed. We feel that we *are* unacceptable. And to feel that is a life-wearying heaviness. Shame-burdened people are the sort whom Jesus had in mind when he invited the "weary and heavy-laden" to trade their heaviness for his lightness.

Whether healthy or unhealthy, true or false, shame is always a heavy feeling of being an unacceptable person, a feeling that, one way or the other, needs healing.

REFLECT: *When you feel the heavy burden of shame, what do you do? How do you find relief from the shame?*

The Irony of Shame

May those who hope in you not be disgraced because of me, O Lord,
the LORD Almighty; may those who seek you not be
put to shame because of me, O God of Israel.

PSALM 69:6

There is a nice irony in shame: our feelings of inferiority are a sure sign of our superiority, and our feelings of unworthiness testify to our great worth. Only a very noble being can feel shame. The reason is simple: a creature meant to be a little less than God is likely to feel a deep dissatisfaction with herself if she falls a notch below the splendid human being she is meant to be. If we never feel shame, we may have lost contact with the person we most truly are. If we can still feel the pain, it is because we are healthy enough to feel uncomfortable with being less than we ought to be and less than we want to be. This is healthy shame.

JOURNAL: *Do a shame audit: Is the shame you've felt lately healthy or unhealthy?*

MONDAY *The Sting of Shame*

> *He who ignores discipline comes to poverty and shame,*
> *but whoever heeds correction is honored.*

PROVERBS 13:18

Shame has no intelligence; it does not reason with us. It is a feeling. However, whenever we feel shame, it sets us at a crossroad. We have a choice: do we rush to get relief, or do we first ask what causes the pain?

To ask why we are feeling the sting of shame is a step into self-understanding. When we probe our shame, we may discover a great deal about ourselves that is worth knowing. What we find out about ourselves may disappoint us deeply. It may also make us feel grateful for the good qualities we had not dared give ourselves credit for before. But whatever there is for us to discover inside ourselves, shame may be the push we need to make us look and see.

JOURNAL: *Think back on your experiences of shame with an eye toward learning what is "worth knowing" about yourself—including the good qualities you may not have dared to give yourself credit for in the past.*

A Good Gift Gone Bad

*See, I lay in Zion a stone that causes men to stumble and a rock that makes them fall,
and the one who trusts in him will never be put to shame.*

ROMANS 9:33

Shame can be like a signal from a drunken signalman who warns of a train that is not coming. The pain of this shame is not a signal of something wrong in us that needs to be made right. Our shame is what is wrong with us. It is a false shame because the feeling has no basis in reality. It is unhealthy shame because it saps our creative powers and kills our joy. It is a shame we do not deserve because we are not as bad as our feelings tell us we are. Undeserved shame is a good gift gone bad.

It makes little difference what we call it—false shame, or unhealthy shame, or undeserved shame. It is all one feeling. The adjectives we give it only reflect its different tones. Whatever we call it, we mean to say that it is a shame we do not deserve to feel.

REFLECT: *What unhealthy shame—the kind that kills your joy—are you carrying these days?*

A Burning Ember

> *I strive always to keep my conscience clear before God and man.*
>
> ACTS 24:16

Shame is a flame from the glowing ember of our original fire. The ember still burns at the core of our lives, still shines in our memories, still glimmers in our hopes, and still invites us to be one with her again.

How does our true self get its message to us? In many ways. Some of us get it straight from our conscience. Some of us get it from the stories of those who went before us. Some of us learn it from what wise and profound minds have taught us. All of us get it because the divine Spirit prods and pushes, nudges and shoves us with intimations of the better self we were created to be.

PRAY: *Ask the Spirit of God to prod, push and nudge you into a greater recognition of who you were created to be.*

Our True Selves in Christ

May my heart be blameless toward your decrees, that I may not be put to shame.

PSALM 119:80

A healthy sense of shame is perhaps the surest sign of our divine origin and our human dignity. When we feel this sense of shame, we are feeling a nudge from our true selves.

Where is this so-called true self? Is it hiding somewhere inside of us, like a forgotten ghost who haunts us with memories of the self we used to be? What is it like? How do we know it when we see it?

Our true self is like the design for a building still under construction or the original design for a building that needs restoring. It is stamped in the depths of us like a template for the selves we are meant to be and yet are failing to be.

Christians recognize the pattern of their true selves in the story of Jesus. We may also recognize it when we see it in the lives of our heroes and saints. We feel it in the pressure we get from our own conscience when it works right. We know it by a deep intuition we have of the better person we would be if we truly were all we could be.

REFLECT: *When have you recently felt a nudge from your true self? What kind of construction (or reconstruction) was it nudging you toward?*

An Integrated Whole

The man of integrity walks securely,
but he who takes crooked paths will be found out.

PROVERBS 10:9

Any image of the true self is blended from many ingredients.

First, your true self is a grateful person. You feel the gladness that comes when you sense that every breath, every heartbeat, every good feeling, every touch of another person's friendly flesh on yours and every loving relationship another person offers you are all wonderful gifts to you.

Second, your true self is an integrated whole. Your life holds together; you are one. You are the same person in secret that you are in public; you have the courage to face unpleasant realities without disguising them; you have a natural bent for accepting and telling the truth even when you pay a price for telling it; and you try to keep your promises even when it costs you some inconvenience and sacrifice. In short, you are a person of integrity.

PRAY: *Ask God to help you be the same person in secret that you are in public, and to have the courage to face the challenges and difficult realities of life.*

A Discerning Person

An angry man stirs up dissension, and a hot-tempered one commits many sins.

PROVERBS 29:22

Your true self is tuned to what is really going on around you—and in you. You listen to the voices, you look at the sights, and you smell the scents of reality all around you. You see things in yourself you are proud of, and you admit to things you feel ashamed of. In short, you are a discerning person.

Your true self is the conductor of your private inner orchestra. You manage your passions. You are not afraid to get angry, but you do not lose control of your temper. You are the sort of person whom other people can count on because you are in charge of your life.

Your true self has a freedom to love with passion. Your love desires all that your loved one can give you, but your love is also a strong desire to give her all she needs from you. You make people better and freer persons for having been loved by you. Your true self is a true lover.

JOURNAL: *Using this week's meditations as your framework, journal your thoughts about your true self in Christ.*

M O N D A Y

The Voice of Grace

My soul is in anguish. How long, O LORD, how long?

PSALM 6:3

A person can catch a healthy case of shame at church. She can also find healing for her shame there. This is the way it should be. The church is meant to be a place where we get the courage to feel some healthy shame and the grace to be healed of it.

But sometimes people come to church carrying a load of unhealthy shame and their burden gets heavier for having come. Their unhealthy shame blocks their spiritual arteries and keeps grace from getting through. And when it finally comes, the word of grace they do hear sounds more like judgment than amazing grace. The sweet hour of prayer becomes an hour of shame.

I remember hearing three voices in the church. Each of them, as I heard it, and each in its own way, fed the shame that I brought with me to church.

The voice of duty: God required me to be perfect before I could be acceptable to him.

The voice of failure: I was flawed, worse than imperfect, and all in all a totally unacceptable human being.

The voice of grace: By the grace of God I could be forgiven for my failure.

REFLECT: *What voices do you hear in your church? What voice do others hear from you? How can your voice convey, to a greater degree, the grace of God?*

A Lightness in Grace

Therefore, since we have been justified through faith,
we have peace with God through our Lord Jesus Christ,
through whom we have gained access by faith into this grace in which we now stand.
And we rejoice in the hope of the glory of God.

ROMANS 5:1-2

Grace, I knew, was good news, but the good news did not feel good to me. The good tidings of great joy made me sad. Grace felt heavy to me.

The good news of grace came only after the bad news that I was mired in sin's clotted clay. I know now what the strategy was: the bad news was meant to get me to feel so hopelessly flawed that I would be that much more grateful for the grace of God when it got to me. But, in fact, my spiritual malaise linked up with my chronic feeling of shame for being human, and the two of them brought forth in me a mess of homogenized shame, healthy and unhealthy, all mixed together. By the time the good word got to me, I was sunk so deep in my shame that I could feel no lightness in grace.

REFLECT: *How would you describe the "good news of grace" in your life? In what ways have you felt the lightness of grace? How can you find a more appropriate balance between the bad news and good news surrounding God's grace?*

The Grace That Saves

In my anguish I cried to the LORD, and he answered by setting me free.

PSALM 118:5

We sang a ditty in Sunday school that went like this:

I've got the joy, joy, joy, joy
Down in my heart,
Down in my heart to stay.

But I did not have it—not to stay, hardly for a moment. What I did have was a chronic case of shame.

Was the shame I felt at church a healthy shame? a shame I deserved? Or was it an unhealthy shame—the kind I didn't deserve? "Was my sinful self my only shame?" No, I was ashamed of my good self too.

My healthy shame and my unhealthy shame were melted down into a glut of unworthiness, and the good word of grace never swam its way into my heart through the spiritual sludge.

I have since learned that the amazing grace that saved a wretch like me brings with it the discovery that I am worthy of the grace that saves.

REFLECT: *"I am worthy of the grace that saves." In what ways is that phrase controversial? In what ways is it empowering?*

Deceiving Ourselves

"Woe to me!" I cried. "I am ruined! For I am a man of unclean lips, and I live among
a people of unclean lips, and my eyes have seen the King, the LORD Almighty."
Then one of the seraphs flew to me with a live coal in his hand, which he had taken with tongs
from the altar. With it he touched my mouth and said, "See, this has touched your lips;
your guilt is taken away and your sin atoned for."

ISAIAH 6:5-7

The capacity for healthy shame is a gift. The experience of unhealthy shame is a curse. We do not deserve it; but we *are* coresponsible for nurturing it into a chronic pain.

No doubt many of us suffer shame we do not deserve because of what other people have done to us. Our parents may have shamed us, and our religious groups may have nurtured what our parents planted. We may also be programmed for shame by our genetic codes. But we are, I believe, responsible for what we do with what other people did to us.

When it comes right down to it, cruel as it sounds, we suffer the shame we do not deserve because we deceive ourselves. We deceive ourselves with the falsehood that we are unworthy human beings. We support our deception with plausible reasons why we *should* feel unworthy. We pollute our consciousness the way a factory manager may release toxic chemicals into a stream and immediately convince himself that the stream is where he *should* release them.

JOURNAL: *Reread the passage from Isaiah 6, and journal your response to the notion that God has taken away your guilt and atoned for your sins.*

Every Mountain Climbed

*Encourage one another daily, as long as it is called Today,
so that none of you may be hardened by sin's deceitfulness.*

HEBREWS 3:13

People who suffer undeserved shame could hear a choir of five hundred voices sing an anthem to their good qualities and deny that they heard a word of it. They hear honest compliments and discount them before they sink in. They tell themselves that people who praise them are not sincere, or that if those people really knew the truth they would not say the nice things they say about them, or that the virtues they praise are really of no account. They always find a way to disqualify whatever good other people see in them.

If they are highly successful people and the evidence of their success is undeniable—no matter what it is they are successful at—they inwardly discount their own success. They discount it because every mountain climbed leaves them with five still to climb. More success will not heal their shame any more than drinking more cola will nourish a starving person.

APPLY: *How do you receive the compliments or praise of others? How can you take more nourishment from such comments?*

Grace and Healing

God . . . has saved us and called us to a holy life—not because of anything
we have done but because of his own purpose and grace.
This grace was given us in Christ Jesus before the beginning of time,
but it has now been revealed through the appearing of our Savior, Christ Jesus.

2 TIMOTHY 1:8-10

Being accepted is the single most compelling need in our lives; no human being can be a friend of herself while at the edges of her consciousness she feels a persistent fear that she may not be accepted by others. Not accepted by what others? By anyone important to us who may size us up and find us wanting. Our parents, our colleagues and bosses, our friends, especially ourselves, and finally our Maker and Redeemer.

Our struggle with shame, then, leaves us with a critical question: are we stuck with our merciless illusion that we need to be acceptable before we can feel accepted? Is there an alternative to the shame-producing ideals of secular culture, graceless religion and unaccepting parents?

There is. It is called grace. Grace is the beginning of our healing because it offers the one thing we need most: to be accepted without regard to whether we are acceptable. Grace stands for gift; it is the gift of being accepted before we become acceptable.

PRAY: *Ask God to help you receive, day by day, the gift of knowing that you are accepted even if you don't feel acceptable.*

M O N D A Y

A Wholesale Acceptance

Grace and peace be yours in abundance
through the knowledge of God and of Jesus our Lord.

2 PETER 1:2

Grace overcomes shame not by uncovering an overlooked cache of excellence in ourselves but simply by accepting us, the whole of us, with no regard to our beauty or our ugliness, our virtue or our vices. We are accepted wholesale. Accepted with no possibility of being rejected. Accepted once and accepted forever. Accepted at the ultimate depth of our being. We are given what we have longed for in every nook and nuance of every relationship.

We are ready for grace when we are bone-tired of our struggle to be worthy and acceptable. After we have tried too long to earn the approval of everyone important to us, we are ready for grace. When we are tired of trying to be the person somebody sometime convinced us we had to be, we are ready for grace. When we have given up all hope of ever being an acceptable human being, we may hear in our hearts the ultimate reassurance: we are accepted, accepted by grace.

JOURNAL: *Write about a time that you felt bone-tired and in need of a touch of God's grace. What happened?*

Graceless Religion

Woe to you, teachers of the law and Pharisees, you hypocrites!
You shut the kingdom of heaven in men's faces. You yourselves do not enter,
nor will you let those enter who are trying to.

MATTHEW 23:13

To be accepted whether or not we deserve to be accepted has always been an outrage to careful and rigid moralists. To the ancient Pharisees, for instance, it looked like the most wicked bargain ever offered to a sucker full of shame. In their straight-line moral bookkeeping there were two kinds of people: people who are acceptable enough to be accepted and people who are not. If you are one of the second kind, too bad for you.

Graceless religion worries that grace will turn a spiritually homeless person into a freeloader. If you can be accepted without being acceptable, why try? It is a fair question.

The answer to the question could begin with a comparison. Who has the better crack at living an acceptable life? A child who is warmly accepted by his parents from the start? Or a child who is abandoned and left with a persuasive hunch that she was rejected because she did not deserve to be accepted?

REFLECT: *Think through the question, "If you can be accepted without being acceptable, why try?"*

Walking Contradictions

You, O LORD, keep my lamp burning; my God turns my darkness into light.

PSALM 18:28

Grace gives us the courage to look at the messy mixture of shadow and light inside our lives, be ashamed of some of what we see, and then accept the good news that God accepts us with our shadows and all the ogres who live inside of them.

None of us is one simple sort of person. What we are is a set of walking contradictions. Dostoyevsky always got at the truth of our contradictions by putting them in their utter extremes. One of his characters, Dmitri Karamazov, groaned that he had both Jezebel the harlot and Mary the virgin inside of him; life would be simpler, he thought, if he could only get rid of one of them.

But our inner lives are not partitioned like day and night, with pure light on one side of us and total darkness on the other. Mostly, our souls are shadowed places; we live at the border where our dark sides block our light and throw shadow over our interior places.

JOURNAL: *Write down your thoughts about the shadows and light inside your own life, and accept the good news that God accepts you.*

The Lightness of Grace

For God so loved the world that he gave his one and only Son,
that whoever believes in him shall not perish but have eternal life.

JOHN 3:16

When grace comes to us graciously, it heals. When grace is offered ungraciously, it shames. You can tell that grace is gracious if it makes you feel better for having it, feel lighter, and, when it comes down to it, feel like the worthy human being you are. The question is: are we accepted by grace only in spite of our unworthiness, or are we also accepted precisely because we are worthy?

A grace that makes us feel worse for having it is an ungracious grace and therefore not really grace at all. If grace heals our shame, it must be a grace that tells us we are worthy to have it. We need, I believe, to recognize that we are accepted not only in spite of our undeserving but because of our worth.

REFLECT: *What does this very familiar passage from John 3:16 mean to you?*

The Victor and the Vanquished

Therefore, as God's chosen people, holy and dearly loved,
clothe yourselves with compassion, kindness, humility, gentleness and patience.

COLOSSIANS 3:12

On a Palm Sunday morning, April 9, 1865, General Robert E. Lee put on his finest dress uniform, mounted Traveller, and rode away from his tired and tattered troops to Appomattox, where he would surrender his beaten army to General Ulysses S. Grant. As Lee rode to meet his conqueror, he fully expected that his men would be herded like cattle into railroad cars and taken to a Union prison and that he, as their general, would be tried and executed as a disgraced traitor.

In the tidy living room of the home where the vanquished and the victor met, Lee asked Grant what his terms of surrender were to be. Grant told Lee that his men were free to take their horses with them and go back to their little farms and that Lee too was free to go home and create a new life. Lee offered Grant his sword; Grant refused it. As he watched General Lee mount Traveller and ride back to his troops, Grant took off his hat and saluted his defeated enemy. It was a gracious grace. And it deeply affected the defeated general: as long as he lived, Lee allowed no critical word of Grant to be spoken in his presence.

REFLECT: *How do you respond to the interaction Grant and Lee had on that Palm Sunday morning? In what way is it an example of compassion, kindness and humility?*

Gambling on Grace

But the father said to his servants, "Quick! Bring the best robe and put it on him.
Put a ring on his finger and sandals on his feet.
Bring the fattened calf and kill it. Let's have a feast and celebrate.
For this son of mine was dead and is alive again;
he was lost and is found." So they began to celebrate.

L U K E   1 5 : 2 2 - 2 4

The prodigal son disowned his father and his family, left the farm in the lurch, went off to a far country and spent his money on good wine and bad women. When he went through his last denarius, he—a Jew—ended up on a hog farm and got so hungry he salivated over the swill he fed the hogs. What he really swallowed was a dose of healthy shame.

So he gambled on his father's grace and headed back home. He did not expect much, but he had no alternative. When his father saw him coming, belly full of shame, the stately old man pulled up his robe above his knees and scrambled out to meet him.

The first thing the shamed prodigal said to his father was, "I don't feel worthy to be called a son; take me on as a hired hand. I'll make my bed in the barn." But his father embraced him, threw a neighborhood party and took him back in the family as a beloved son.

REFLECT: *As you read the parable of the prodigal son, with whom do you most identify?*

MONDAY

Amazing Grace

Live lives worthy of God, who calls you into his kingdom and glory.

1 THESSALONIANS 2:12

No matter who sings our folk hymn to grace—a choir of prisoners in the state penitentiary, folks down on their luck, the rejected and despised, or high-placed guests at a presidential breakfast—all of us feel less like wretches for singing it. When I sing "Amazing Grace," I feel a worth inside me that tells me I am a better person than the wretch whom only grace could save. This is the sweet, sweet irony of the grace that saves a wretch like me: it is a most gracious grace that tells me I am worth it.

REFLECT: *How does the singing of "Amazing Grace," or hymns and praise songs with similar themes, affect you?*

Moses said to the LORD, "O Lord, I have never been eloquent,
neither in the past nor since you have spoken to your servant.
I am slow of speech and tongue." The LORD said to him, "Who gave man his mouth?
Who makes him deaf or mute? Who gives him sight or makes him blind? Is it not I, the LORD?"

EXODUS 4:10-11

Shame and pride are opposite feelings about ourselves. Shame—the feeling of being unworthy and unacceptable—is the loss of pride. As shame is healed, we find our pride again.

My mother could abide no pride. She could not abide it in poor people with big ideas or in rich people with big heads. She could not abide it in the proud way some people walk.

When I arrived in high school, I was a skinny rail taller than six feet. I usually drooped into a slouch to make myself an inch shorter than the lank spindle I was. My speech teacher noticed me one day and took me aside. "Lewis," she said, her eyes climbing up to meet mine, "you are lucky to be tall. Walk straight; be proud of your height." I dropped my slouch and slipped into a strut on the spot. When I strutted home my mother caught me at it: "Oh, Lewis, Lewis, Lewis, you must not walk so proud."

What my mother had against pride was that humility was safer.

PRAY: *Ask God to help you heal unhealthy shame and recover a sense of healthy pride and humility.*

Applauding Excellence

With your help I can advance against a troop; with my God I can scale a wall.

2 SAMUEL 22:30

A person who has experienced grace knows that what she is and what she has are gifts from God, so when she feels pride, she feels gratitude with the same impulse. We could put the difference between graceless arrogance and grace-based pride this way: arrogance is pride without gratitude, while grace-given pride is nothing but gratitude. A person with hubris thinks he is God. A person with grace-based pride thanks his God.

Grace-based pride is a kind of elation, especially about something we have accomplished. When we feel elation, we simply must share it; we have to show somebody what we have done so they can share our pride.

I see it in a child who has just tied her shoestring for the first time or turned a somersault: "Mommy, Mommy, look! Watch me. No, Mother, stop talking and come look." She feels what I suppose the Creator felt after he made himself a fine world. When he saw how well he had done, he created some people who could share the world he was so proud of having made. Excellence cries for applause.

PRAY: *Pause to pray in gratitude for God's grace in giving you gifts and talents.*

The Appearance of Joy

But let all who take refuge in you be glad; let them ever sing for joy.
Spread your protection over them, that those who love your name may rejoice in you.

PSALM 5:11

As we gain the freedom to accept ourselves, we can be reasonably sure that we are healed of shame. Accepting ourselves is difficult. It is not a one-shot cure. It is rather like a long and wonderful passage. We accept ourselves when we take responsibility for writing our life stories out of whatever raw materials we were given. We do it when we own the depths of ourselves even when what is going on down there scares us some. We do it when we take a grateful pride in what we do with our lives, in snippets or in full cloth. These are the makings of self-acceptance. They are the warm-ups for the appearance of joy.

JOURNAL: *Write down your musings on the elements of grateful pride in your life. In what ways do they serve as warm-ups for the appearance of joy?*

Keeping Our Commitments

Woe to you, teachers of the law and Pharisees, you hypocrites!
You clean the outside of the cup and dish,
but inside they are full of greed and self-indulgence.

MATTHEW 23:25

Some people sweat and snort through daily workouts so that they will be fit enough to sweat and snort through the workouts. "Why do you jog?" I asked my perspiring friend. "To keep fit," he answered. "And why do you want to keep fit?" I asked. "So that I can be in shape to jog," he replied. Good enough reason for fanatics, I suppose.

But surely we are not bound to commitments so that we can get in shape to keep our commitments—so that, in turn, we can look good to the connoisseurs of virtue.

Becoming jut-jawed persons who preen themselves on their moral luster is not the reward we get for sticking to commitments. The reward for commitment keeping is a better kind of life for people who care about each other.

REFLECT: *How would you describe the reward for keeping commitments? Why is it important in the life of the believer?*

The Woman of the Pharisees

Woe to you, teachers of the law and Pharisees, you hypocrites!
You give a tenth of your spices—mint, dill and cummin.
But you have neglected the more important matters of the law—justice, mercy and faithfulness.
You should have practiced the latter, without neglecting the former.

MATTHEW 23:23

Something almost always goes wrong when we keep our commitments out of commitment to our own commitment keeping. French novelist Francois Mauriac tells a story about someone he had the inspiration to call *The Woman of the Pharisees*. This woman, the grande dame of the valley, very rich in houses and land, was committed to the poor people in her village, visiting them all regularly, always leaving behind a gift suitable to their needs—as she saw them—along with a suggestion that a little more ambition and a little more thrift could improve their situation. She never left a poor family's house without making them feel worse for her having been there. She flogged them with her commitment to them. And they hated her for the gifts almost as much as they hated themselves for accepting them. What she was committed to was her reputation as a rich woman committed to poor people.

JOURNAL: *How do you respond to the story from Francois Mauriac's novel? Journal your thoughts.*

M O N D A Y

Small Islands of Security

All of you, as responsible to God, should remain in the situation in which God called you.

1 CORINTHIANS 7:24 TNIV

What makes commitment keeping worth working at it is this: It serves the long-term good of people in relationship, people who want to live in a caring human community. That's the beginning and the end of it. We can create a good life together only out of trust. And trust, to make it last, needs commitment.

We need to know that people who promise to be with us are really going to be there. If we all lived as strictly free-floating, unfettered, self-enhancing individuals, we would all be left hanging in the vacuum of each other's undependability. We need something firmer.

Commitments give it to us. They create small islands of security for us in our oceans of insecurity. They make enclaves of steadiness in the jungles of change. They give us the only human basis for trusting each other. For counting on each other.

JOURNAL: *Consider the commitments you have made to God and to others. In what ways have you remained steady in your commitments? In what ways have you not?*

The Importance of Community

Since we have these promises, dear friends, let us purify ourselves from everything that contaminates body and spirit, perfecting holiness out of reverence for God.

2 CORINTHIANS 7:1

Commitment is the invisible fiber that binds a collection of individuals into a caring community. A large one or a small one. Everything depends on it. Everything from a family reunion to a concord of nations, from calling a committee meeting to founding a nation, from celebrating communion to getting a return trip ticket to Pasadena. Not to mention a lasting marriage. Or a good friendship.

Maybe you can have a regime or a gang or a crowd or a prison full of inmates or even a foreign legion without commitment, but you cannot have a human community. The only way we can anywhere, anytime, create a good human relationship within a caring community is by daring to make and caring to keep commitments to each other.

The reason for keeping our commitments to each other is that, in the long run, keeping commitments is the only way to have a community, and as T. S. Eliot reminded us, there is no human life that is not lived in human community.

REFLECT: *In what ways are you experiencing community? How have your commitments to others affected your ability to relate in community?*

Writing Our Stories

Be devoted to one another in brotherly love.
Honor one another above yourselves.

ROMANS 12:10

We are all writing our stories, and each of us has to write his or her own. I cannot write my parents' stories, any more than they could have written mine. I cannot write my children's stories, though there have been times that I have wanted to. I can write only mine.

The trick is to write a continuing story. A story with a plot that has a central character. Not a collection of unconnected episodes about a collection of unconnected characters.

Writing a continuing story out of my life depends on whether I dare to make commitments to people and care enough to keep the commitments I make. And whether I accept other people's commitments to me as gifts that contribute to my story.

In fact, who we are always begins with somebody's commitment to us.

PRAY: *Ask God to help you keep your commitments to him, to family and to others, and to grow in an awareness of your continuing story.*

Discriminating Friendship

Now that you have purified yourselves by obeying the truth so that you have sincere love for your brothers, love one another deeply, from the heart.

1 PETER 1 : 2 2

We all want someone who knows us better than anyone else does and yet accepts us, enjoys us, needs us, holds nothing back from us, keeps our secrets and is there for us when we want to be near her.

We all seem to need at least one close friend. Even people who believe they ought to love everybody need special people they want to be close to just because they like them. And are liked by them. It's different from charity; we ought to feel charity for needy people. But we want somebody as a close friend because we like her, not because she needs our kindness.

It's a matter of preference. A close friend is somebody who prefers to have us around, is partial to us, makes us his favorite. We talk about things together we don't talk about with other people. We do things together that we don't want to do with anyone else, least not as much as we want to do them with each other. Friends stick with their favorites; that's the way of friendship: it always discriminates.

REFLECT: *Who is a special, close friend in your life? In what ways can you invest in that friendship today or this week?*

Three Kinds of Friendship

No one has ever seen God; but if we love one another,
God lives in us and his love is made complete in us.

1 JOHN 4:12

What goes into the making of any friendship? What are the ingredients that mesh ordinary people into this wonderful, this tender, this too-fragile relationship? And why can't we count on it to last?

There are three kinds of friendship, as Aristotle saw it. One of them is a friendship based on affection: Friends like each other and enjoy each other. Another is a friendship based on usefulness: Friends do things for each other. And a third kind is based on character: Friends admire each other.

I think every real friendship is a mixture of all three ingredients. It's just that the blend changes from one friendship to another. But there is a lot to say for Aristotle's list, enough anyway to see why none of his three kinds of friendship can last long if it doesn't have commitment as the bonding agent.

REFLECT: *Think about the close friendships you have enjoyed over the years. How has your commitment to those friendships contributed to their longevity?*

The Character of Commitment

A man of many companions may come to ruin,
but there is a friend who sticks closer than a brother.

P R O V E R B S   1 8 : 2 4

We don't usually begin a friendship with a commitment. The commitment comes to life gradually. We commit ourselves to each other in snippets, in all sorts of little ways, over the long haul.

We hardly notice when we have first made a commitment to be a friend to someone. But when our friends have special needs or get into tough situations, we discover that we actually have made a commitment to them without thinking much about it. What sort of commitment is it? I think we make three sorts of commitments, and these are fundamental for lasting friendships.

Commitment is about loyalty. We don't betray friends; we don't treat them the way people treat enemies. *Commitment is about caring.* Caring for a friend is the heart of commitment. To care is to invest oneself in a friend's fortune. *Commitment is about accepting a friend's claim on us.* A friend has a right to expect us to do things for her that we would not do for just anyone.

J O U R N A L : *Who in your life embody the threefold character of loyalty, caring and claim? How do these relationships reflect the character of Christ.*

M O N D A Y *The Hope of Hope Itself*

> *Let us hold unswervingly to the hope we profess,*
> *for he who promised is faithful.*

Commitments are a chancy thing in the best of times. But right now, in our kind of world, the only hope is hope itself.

Do we believe that God is committed to us? Is he committed to keeping our world a place where making commitments to each other works? If God is really committed to us and to our important personal relationships, we have reason for hope and a reason for making commitments to them. So in my own experience, because I do believe in God, I have to ask whether my faith really does give me hope that keeping commitments is still the only way to keep our deepest human relationships alive and creative.

PRAY: *Pray that the Spirit of God will help you hold unswervingly to hope, and to the commitments you've made to him and to others.*

No Guarantees

> *Now faith is being sure of what we hope for*
> *and certain of what we do not see.*

HEBREWS 11:1

Hope is not a guarantee of complete satisfaction. It is a kind of power, an inner power to believe that life can get better, not perfect, just better than it is—good enough to make it worth the struggle to keep our commitment to someone about whom we care.

In fact, we are better equipped to keep our commitments if we come to terms with the likelihood that some things don't change.

Let's think a moment about things that don't change. You used to be twenty-five, now you're forty-five; you can't go back, no use hoping. You've had a mastectomy and lost a breast; you can't get it back. Your husband has incurable erotic burnout; he won't ever be as attractive as the suave charmer at your office. Your wife is a messy housekeeper and a lousy cook and she just doesn't think those things are important, even though they mean a lot to you; she probably isn't going to change. Your children have flown the coop and left you alone with your workaholic husband; they won't come back, not to stay.

Hope that things can change is not a blank check drawn on earthly perfection. Coping with what is may be a realist's way of hoping for what can be.

REFLECT: *How do you maintain faith and hope in something you do not see?*

For God did not send his Son into the world to condemn the world,
but to save the world through him.

JOHN 3:17

Ultimately, the question of hope gets us to the question of God and of whether he is committed to us. Will God be there for us? Does he personally care enough to keep a commitment to people who wonder what the odds of making it are?

No matter what our faith or doubt or disbelief may be, the ultimate question is whether God is committed to us.

My fascination with the question of whether God is really up there cools down quickly if I cannot believe he is committed to me down here—and to others, to weak, needy, faulty people like me. But in those moments when the current of his committed presence flows into my weakness, his reality becomes ultimately important to me.

JOURNAL: *Do you believe that God is committed to you? that he will be there for you? What is the basis for your belief?*

An Escape into Freedom

Moses thought, "I will go over and see this strange sight—why the bush does not burn up."

EXODUS 3:3

It helps to know that people with a lot more faith than I have sometimes wondered whether they could depend on God's commitment. Biblical stories are often the best. Take the one about Moses and his surprising experience with the burning bush.

Moses, who had been brought up in the Egyptian Pharaoh's court, was living in exile at the time, a fugitive from Pharaoh—and, for that matter, from his own people—when God spotted him alone in the wilderness, tending his father-in-law's sheep. God flagged him down with a burning piece of chaparral that flamed oddly long. Moses went to take a second look, out of mere curiosity, but it was not what he saw, it was what he heard that shifted the winds of the future. God had come back.

The Lord was committed to renewing his relationship with the human family, and he wanted Moses to go back to Egypt, where the Hebrews had been slaves for four centuries, and prepare them for escape into freedom and a new commitment to God.

S T U D Y : *Reread the entire third chapter of Exodus. How does the story of God's commitment to and interaction with Moses give you hope?*

The Secret of Commitment

> How good and pleasant it is
> when God's people live together in unity! . . .
> For there the LORD bestows his blessing,
> even life forevermore.

PSALM 133 TNIV

Out of my private struggles with despair, I have come to see that hope is the final secret of all commitment.

When two people are committed to each other, when the innerspring of their commitment is care, each for the other, there are possibilities in the toughest situations. Not certainties. But possibilities. Not possibilities of things being all we've ever wanted them to be. But possibilities of things becoming better than they are. Good enough to make the future together, as friends, as partners, as family, better for having kept on caring for each other just a little more than we care for ourselves.

REFLECT: *In what ways do your deep, abiding friendships provide an innerspring of care to help you through the toughest situations? In what ways are you providing that innerspring to others?*

Coping with Suffering

For he has not despised or disdained the suffering of the afflicted one;
he has not hidden his face from him but has listened to his cry for help.

PSALM 22:24

Love is an uncommon power to cope with common suffering. Suffering itself takes no talent. It comes to us, takes us captive, pins us down. We are all its victims. Some of us have to suffer more than others. Some are able to suffer with more grace than others. But it is love that enables us to suffer long.

To suffer long seems like a grim return on love. Love, it would seem, holds a poor hand if long-suffering is one of its best cards. But in a world where suffering is almost a law of life, the power to suffer long may be one of life's most needed gifts.

What all suffering really comes down to is the experience of anything we want very much not to experience. The key here is the phrase "very much." To qualify as sufferers, we must want to be rid of something with such passion that it hurts.

JOURNAL: *Reread Psalm 22:24 and reflect on the psalmist's promise of God's presence in the midst of affliction. Journal your thoughts or if you prefer, turn the passage into a prayer, thanking God for his presence and for listening to your cry for help in times of need.*

MONDAY *God's Love Song*

> And now these three remain: faith, hope and love.
> But the greatest of these is love.

1 CORINTHIANS 13:13

Long-suffering is the power to be a creative victim. Long-suffering is not passive. It is a tough, active, aggressive style of life. It takes power of soul to be long-suffering. God's love song is not in praise of merely hanging on. It is in praise of power, the power of affirming and creating life in the midst of suffering.

The power to do this is *agapic* love. *Agape* is the love modeled by God in his relations with sinners, the love that drove Jesus to the cross. *Agapic* love is the liberating power that moves us toward our neighbor with no demand for rewards. Do not ask whether you are able to love without thought of reward. Just understand that God's love is the power to move us in that direction.

APPLY: *Look for opportunities today to love others with no requirement of reward in return. If you find this challenging, remember that God's love can move you in that direction.*

Then Jesus went with his disciples to a place called Gethsemane,
and he said to them, "Sit here while I go over there and pray."
He took Peter and the two sons of Zebedee along with him,
and he began to be sorrowful and troubled.

MATTHEW 26:36-37

Agape is born of divine strength; therefore, it has the power to be creatively weak. Because it is not driven by ardent need, it has power to wait. It gives power to accept life, to find goodness in living while we are victims of situations we despise. This is the only way to explain two attitudes we observe in Jesus toward his own horrible suffering. In Gethsemane we hear him plead with God to be spared the cross that lies ahead. The reality of his suffering is seen in the fact that he did not want the pain. The next day, as he bears his cross to Calvary, he tells the weeping women who follow him, "Don't cry for me." Here we see his power to affirm himself as the loving Lord and free Savior who chose to suffer, chose to be a victim of suffering. He was not a helpless victim of tragedy; he was a powerful person who chose to be weak. He had the strength to become a victim even while he affirmed his own life as free in obedience to love.

JOURNAL: *Looking once again at the passage on Christ in the garden of Gethsemane, contemplate the notion that Jesus had the strength to choose to suffer in obedience to the love of the Father. What does this say about how much he loves you?*

The Road to Justice

*I know that the LORD secures justice for the poor
and upholds the cause of the needy.*

PSALM 140:12

Love is the power to suffer evil for a long time, but it does not drive us to accept the evil we suffer. To suffer evil takes patience and courage. To accept evil is to capitulate to it in order to escape its horror. Long-suffering is a power developed within reality. Accepting evil is a denial of reality.

Martin Luther King asked his people to suffer long on the painful road to justice. He asked them to suffer bricks and bullets, humiliation and intimidation. He asked them to suffer injustice, but he never asked them to accept injustice nor mute their demands for justice *now*. When black people sang "We shall overcome *someday*," they were giving testimony to their long-suffering, but they were not admitting a willingness to accept injustice until that day. They were asked to accept unjust persons in love. They were not asked to accept the injustice inflicted by unjust people.

PRAY: *Ask God to give you the power and courage to be long-suffering, while never accepting evil.*

Be strong and courageous. Do not be afraid or terrified because of them,
for the LORD your God goes with you; he will never leave you nor forsake you.

DEUTERONOMY 31:6

When we have the patience to accept ourselves, to accept our future in life, in the face of deep loss or persistent frustration, we are living in love's power. When we have learned to believe that our lives have meaning, when we have opened our hearts to some feelings of joy, when we have seen some rays of light that make us glad, we are long-suffering.

Then courage is added to patience. Courage is the power to resist assaults on our lives—both negatively and positively. In a negative sense, courage is the power to be angry at—indeed, to hate—the evil that assaults us. The person with cancer needs courage to hate the disease that is sapping away his life. The person struck by loss of sight needs courage to hate blindness.

But then, positively, love comes in, at this moment, as the power to suffer long what we desperately want to go away. Love is the courage to love life and be glad for it. Love is the courage to discover that life is not completely tied to the precious goods we have lost or have not yet found. God's love song does not hammer at us with a demand to be more courageous. This would only defeat us. It says that, with God, there is the power. Its name is love.

REFLECT: *How is the love of God giving you courage to suffer long what you desperately want to go away?*

A Redemptive "Yes!"

The Lord is not slow in keeping his promise, as some understand slowness.
He is patient with you, not wanting anyone to perish, but everyone to come to repentance.

2 PETER 3:9

God's love is his Yes to a lost world. It is a redemptive Yes, not merely an indifferent or indulgent one. It is a Yes burning with desire for our salvation. An apostle once wrote a letter to some Christians tempted to read God's long-suffering as divine indifference. Skeptics were arguing that love's long-suffering looked more like forgetfulness than patience. "Why does he wait? History just keeps blundering along as it always has. The pain, the violence, the inhumanity—nothing really changes. Surely, his promise is phony." The writer gives the real reason for God's delay: "God is not willing that any should perish, but that all should come to repentance" (see 2 Peter 3:9). Agape always creates room for reconciliation by suffering long even with what it hates.

PRAY: *In thanksgiving, acknowledge God's great gift of salvation through Christ. In adoration, thank God for his reconciling work through Christ our Lord.*

The Strength of Kindness

But the fruit of the Spirit is love, joy, peace, patience, kindness, goodness, faithfulness, gentleness and self-control. Against such things there is no law.

GALATIANS 5:22-23

Our world cannot understand that love is power and that kindness is the work of that power. The German philosopher Nietzsche hated Christianity for encouraging kindness. He accused Christian love of draining strong people by making them kind, driving them to waste their energies on lepers, cripples and oppressed people. Thus, love weakened the strong of the human race by turning them toward kindness. Were we to rid the world of faith in Christ, and thus of love, he prophesied, we might again produce supermen. The strong could get stronger and the weak die out.

How wrong Nietzsche was! And how wrong are people today who think along such lines. Far from being weakness, kindness is enormous strength— more than most of us have, except now and then. Kindness is the power that moves us to support and heal someone who offers nothing in return. Kindness is the power to move self-centered ego toward the weak, the ugly, the hurt, and to move that ego to invest itself in personal care with no expectation of reward.

REFLECT: *Do you think of kindness as a sign of strength or weakness? If kindness, as the Galatians passage suggests, is one of the fruits of the Spirit, how do we cultivate it?*

M O N D A Y

An Indiscriminate Kindness

Love never fails.

1 CORINTHIANS 13:8

The ultimate model of powerful kindness is God. He has no need to exploit the weak to increase his power. He does not have to be stimulated to greater power by the competitive energies of colleagues or the combatant forces of evil. God is self-generating power.

For this reason, he has the power to be indiscriminate in his kindness. Since he is not kind in order to get a return on his benevolence, he can be kind to the ungrateful and the selfish (Luke 6:35). The Bible stresses his impartiality: "he makes his sun rise on the evil and the good, and sends rain on the just and unjust" (see Matthew 5:45). God's benevolence is uncalculating because it derives from his own power of love. Neither payment for human virtue, nor enticement for human applause, it is the self-generative power of selfless, giving love.

JOURNAL: *Consider journaling a list of the kindness of God evident in your own spiritual journey, your reading of Scripture, and your reflections on the Son of God.*

> *But God chose the foolish things of the world to shame the wise;*
> *God chose the weak things of the world to shame the strong.*

1 CORINTHIANS 1:27

Kindness is a power born of love. Love is the power of God exercised in apparent weakness. The only way to keep kindness alive in the world where obvious power is prized most is to come back to the cross of Christ, where divine power healed the world by becoming weak within the world. At that focal moment of human history, utter weakness was utter redemptive power. The kindness of Christ's cross looks like weakness because it is tender, vulnerable, asks nothing, gives everything, stoops personally to those who are weakest and poorest and ugliest But it is divine power.

Love moved God to become a person like us. Love led him, as a man, to use his power wholly as servant-power. In love's power he gave himself as kindness. He washed dirty feet, wept with grief-wracked people, empathized with a harlot, entered the lives of the disowned and disdained. All his life he was *powerful* in kindness.

PRAY: *Spend some time in prayer, reflecting on the servant-power and servant-kindness shown on Calvary. In response, thank God for the redemptive work of the cross.*

Jealousy and Envy

I am afraid that when I come I may not find you as I want you to be,
and you may not find me as you want me to be.
I fear that there may be quarreling, jealousy, outbursts of anger, factions,
slander, gossip, arrogance and disorder.

2   C O R I N T H I A N S   1 2 : 2 0

Jealousy and envy are different feelings. A student feels no jealousy of the teacher's knowledge; a student feels jealousy when a roommate consistently gets A's while he manages only B's. A merely competent violinist has no jealousy of a Yehudi Menuhin. She feels jealousy when another competent violinist is moved to a higher position in the orchestra than she. We envy without pain. Jealousy is the pain we feel when our role, our position, is threatened by someone close to us. Envy can stimulate us to try harder. Jealousy stimulates us only to resentment of the person who does better.

REFLECT: *When have you felt jealous of another? What was (or is) at the root of the jealousy? How did you resolve it?*

> *May the Lord make your love increase and overflow for each other*
> *and for everyone else, just as ours does for you.*

1 THESSALONIANS 3:12

Love is the inner power to be happy when someone else shares your friend. Love is the power to rejoice in the superior talent, success or power of someone close to you. Indeed, love is the power to be glad when another person shares a part of your loved one's life that you cannot share.

Love as the power to share persons originates in a God who could give his Son to win many sons and daughters who would love each other as well as him. Such love knows that sharing a friend is not losing one but only making the circle a little larger. It knows that another person's excellence does not diminish my own or your own, but only adds to the luster of all.

To be loved with this love and to share its power is to overcome fear—even the fear of loss, even the fear of being left out. In other words, this love enables us to transcend jealousy. It overcomes fear as it overcomes self-pity and the insecurity and suspicion of erotic love. So, this love is the power of sharing without being threatened.

REFLECT: *How do you respond when someone around you achieves success or gains recognition? Are you able to share in the joy, or do you have a sense of being left out?*

Creating Our Images

Ben-Hadad sent another message to Ahab: "May the gods deal with me,
be it ever so severely, if enough dust remains in Samaria to give each of my men a handful."
The king of Israel answered, "Tell him: 'One who puts on his armor
should not boast like one who takes it off.'"

1 KINGS 20:10-11

Boasting is our private advertising business, our little campaign to publicize an *image* of ourselves. Sometimes we boast because we suspect that people will not care enough to notice us or be shrewd enough to recognize our assets. Other times we boast out of a fear that our assets are not worth their caring. Anyway we don't trust things to take their course, to make the proverbial better mousetrap and wait for the world to beat a path to our door. We have to create our image and put it up front in our ego's display case. This is boasting.

Not that there is anything wrong with wanting to be noticed, wanting people to applaud you or buy your mousetrap. But there is something wrong about boasting, and that is that it *always* distorts reality. We boast when we are afraid that, if people do notice us, they will not admire what they see.

PRAY: *Pray that God would fill you with a sense of worth and such an awareness of his love that you will not be tempted to utilize the private advertising business of boasting.*

The Dynamics of Pride

For it is by grace you have been saved, through faith—and this not from yourselves,
it is the gift of God—not by works, so that no one can boast. For we are God's workmanship,
created in Christ Jesus to do good works, which God prepared in advance for us to do.

EPHESIANS 2:8-10

The root cause of arrogance is pride, but between the two stands vanity. Pride leaves us vain, and vanity pushes us toward arrogance. The dynamics of this involve three sets of persons. We begin with pride toward God. Pride leaves us with vanity inside ourselves. And vanity pushes us into arrogance toward other people.

Pride is arrogance in a vertical direction. Spiritual pride has to do with how we feel about God. Pride in the religious sense is an arrogant refusal to let God be God. It is to grab God's status for oneself. In the vivid language of the Bible, pride is puffing yourself up in God's face. Pride is turning down God's invitation to join the dance of life as a creature in his garden and wishing instead to be the Creator, independent, reliant on one's own resources. Never does pride want to *pray* for strength, ask for grace, plead for mercy or give thanks to God. Pride is the grand illusion, the fantasy of fantasies, the cosmic put-on.

APPLY: *Asking for God's grace to do so, seek to cultivate the discipline of authentic Christian humility, eschewing the great sin of pride. Ask a trusted friend today to help you guard against vanity and arrogance.*

MONDAY

Justice in Heaven and on Earth

A generous man will himself be blessed, for he shares his food with the poor.

PROVERBS 22:9

Love, as the self-giving power of a just God, *seeks* justice. For love can do no less than see that our neighbor gets what is rightfully his. Love is ready to do more, but it cannot do less. Anyone who says that lovers need not care about justice is talking nonsense. How can we want to meet our neighbor's need unless we want him to have what is his by right?

God's love song, however, tells us that love does not move us to seek justice for *ourselves*. This is the catch. Love will drive us to move heaven and earth to seek justice for others. Love may lead us to take up arms and overthrow tyrants for the sake of justice for tyranny's victims. It may drive us to the Supreme Court for the sake of justice for others. Love may send us into the streets to throw a community into turmoil for the sake of justice for the oppressed people. But love does *not* move us a millimeter to seek justice for ourselves. "Love does not seek its own."

JOURNAL: *Take time to journal the ways in which you can join with your neighbors, your church community, coworkers or family to very practically seek justice in your local area, your nation or the global community.*

The Personal Power to Discern

I am your servant; give me discernment that I may understand your statutes.

PSALM 119:125

Being willing to sacrifice our rights is one thing; knowing *when* is another. Love needs the sensitive gift of *discernment*. No built-in computer calculates for us the right time to fight and the right time to surrender. God did not provide a manual that tells us which way to go when love and justice pull in opposite directions. The secret of knowing lies with the personal power to discern. Discernment is the ability to see the difference between things. It is the power to see what is really happening, to see what is really important and what is not important. Discernment is insight—the power to see *inside* of things. It is the strange and subtle ability to see beneath the surface, to sense the personal factors of any situation and to grasp what spiritual issues are really at stake. When we are directly involved, discernment is insight into the mixture of motives moving our own hearts. Working its way though real life, love needs the gift of discernment to focus its drive toward others in helping service.

PRAY: *Pray for the ability to see ways you can make a difference in the life of another.*

Our Hearts Are Deceitful

For this reason, since the day we heard it, we have not ceased praying for you
and asking that you may be filled with the knowledge of God's will
in all spiritual wisdom and understanding.

COLOSSIANS 1:9 NRSV

Discernment is an answer to prayer. St. Paul tells us he prayed that his fellow Christians would be "filled with the knowledge of God's will in all spiritual wisdom and understanding." He was praying, I take it, for discernment. For what is spiritual wisdom but the power to make sound judgments about spiritual things? Spiritual wisdom helps us decide when to speak and when to keep silent, when to act and when to wait, when to fight and when to surrender. Spiritual wisdom—fallible and subjective—is the power to know what is really going on when others are camouflaging the issues. And it is the power to know what is really going on inside our own hearts. The Bible tells us our hearts are very deceitful (Jeremiah 17:9), and that not even love makes them wholly trustworthy. Hence, what we need in the life of love is the gift of discernment, or spiritual wisdom. For this we can only pray; when it is given, we must use it boldly.

REFLECT: *How do you cultivate spiritual wisdom in your life? What are fresh, life-giving ways you can seek to grow in spiritual wisdom during this season of life?*

The World Is a Gift

Come and see what God has done, how awesome his works in man's behalf!

PSALM 66:5

God comes to us as freely as the wind; once having come, he opens our eyes to a new world. It is a new world to us because we see it in a new way. No longer is the world around us an obstacle course we must run to achieve our reward of happiness. Our environment is not a maze that we must puzzle out successfully or be damned forever. The world is a gift, a playground where we discover our very selves as gifts of God. The first breath of the morning, the first handshake from a friend, the first "good morning" from a spouse, the chance to be healthy, the opportunity to work—all of it a gift from God!

P R A Y : *Thank God for the breath of the new morning, for the sunset this evening and for the joy of life between.*

Overcoming Resentment

> *By this all men will know that you are my disciples,*
> *if you love one another.*
>
> JOHN 13:35

Why do we take the past into our minds and lock it there to keep it alive? Why do we prolong the hurts we receive instead of remembering only the joys of the past? We remember the hurts so that we can enjoy the pain of yesterday over and over again. We keep it alive for the pleasure we can get from our resentment against the one who hurt us.

Love alone has the power to release memory's grip on yesterday's evil, for only love is the power that moves us toward people without expectation of return and therefore with great tolerance for hurt. Love does not demand explanations and apologies or keep accounts. Love does not take pleasure in remembering how much we have coming from people who hurt us. For love is the power whose only direction is the help, healing and salvation of the other person. This is why love has the power to overcome resentment.

JOURNAL: *What are your earliest recollections of joy as a child? as a young adult? What brings you whispers of joy today?*

Our Model of Love

Dear friends, since God so loved us, we also ought to love one another.

1 JOHN 4:11

God's love is our model. It keeps coming to us though we have fed a thousand offenses into his memory bank. God's love is also our power. We are enabled by a love that keeps no accounts since they were settled by Christ at his cross. From the cross, God moves on to new history. He does not wait until we have sifted and weighed all our faults. In love, he begins where we are. Moved by this love, we have no need to savor past hurts caused by old enemies. Our ego has no need to nourish resentment, for it is supported not by staying on top of personal relations but by accepting forgiveness and freedom from God. We lose our masochistic taste for angry memories of the wrongs others have inflicted on us. We do not need to keep accurate score, for we do not need to be a moral winner. We forgive and start anew with what we now are and with what the other person now is.

REFLECT: *When you read that accounts were "settled by Christ at his cross," how do you respond? If we fully embrace that notion, how would it impact the way we respond when other people wound us?*

M O N D A Y *Love's Ultimate Goal*

For if you forgive men when they sin against you,
your heavenly Father will also forgive you.

MATTHEW 6:14

The person with the power to forget is the person who can bring others around to doing the same. Able to start fresh for himself, leaving past history's confusion tangled, he can carry on Christ's own ministry of reconciliation. He learns how to help people wipe from the record book all the old scores they have kept against each other. Love is that person's power. Love is the power that drives us toward the *other* who has done us wrong because it is able to tear up every moral scorecard. This is reconciliation, and reconciliation is love's ultimate goal.

PRAY: *Ask God to help you to be a part of his ministry of reconciliation in the world today.*

Matching God's Purpose

Jesus answered, "I am the way and the truth and the life.
No one comes to the Father except through me.

JOHN 14:6

We can say three things about what the Bible means by truth. First, truth is larger than accurate statements, correct figures and consistent reasoning. Second, truth refers to reality: things are true when they are right, what they ought to be and where they ought to be in relation to each other. Truth is reality when it matches God's purpose. Third, truth is a person, a person whose acts and words blend to draw a profile of human life as God meant it to be lived. In this way, Jesus could say, "I am the truth." When one meets Jesus as truth, he learns what God has in mind for human life, what reality is meant to be on earth.

REFLECT: *Reflect on the three dimensions of truth put forth above. How can the believer "meet Jesus as truth" today, more than two thousand years after his death and resurrection?*

Love's Patience

Love is patient, love is kind. It does not envy, it does not boast, it is not proud.
It is not rude, it is not self-seeking, it is not easily angered, it keeps no record of wrongs.

1 CORINTHIANS 13:4-5

Realism is the secret of love's patience. Love is not idealism; it does not have to be fanatic. It is not hysterical; it knows the world is not going to fall apart if we don't immediately clean up every mess. Love's patience is no mush fantasy that people are all really very nice. Love knows that we live in a mixture of good and evil. Love knows that life now is ambiguous. But love can bear it. Love can even rejoice in this mixed-up life because it rejoices with the truth, the Truth who will "reconcile all things to himself" (see Colossians 1:20) and thus make the world *true* again. Love manages well in a world like ours; but love never approves of the evil that makes our good world the mixed reality it is.

PRAY: *Pray for the ability to offer and receive love and rejoice even in the midst of the mixed-up world, full of ambiguity and good and evil.*

Bearing Our Condemnation

Therefore, there is now no condemnation for those who are in Christ Jesus.

ROMANS 8:1

Knowing people, God realized that we could not manage our burdens alone. Being love, he was moved to carry them with us. "Surely he has borne our griefs and carried our sorrows" (see Isaiah 53:4). God joined us on earth as burden-carrier, even to the extent of carrying the burden of being in the wrong: "he bore the sin of many" (Isaiah 53:12). God became a burden-bearer *with* us. But he did not relieve us of responsibility for our burdens. Though he bore our griefs, we still have griefs to carry. He carried our guilt, but we still have guilt to bear. The cross was not an end to human sorrow, nor Jesus' death the death of human guilt. How, then, does God's love really bear our burden?

Love's sacrifice carried away judgment. Christ bore our condemnation. The art of living with God now is the art of accepting guilt without accepting judgment and condemnation for it. It is an art that anyone can learn once opened to the love that moved Christ to bear guilt *with* us and judgment *for* us.

PRAY: *Ask God to help you learn the art of accepting guilt for your actions while being free of judgment through the grace of Jesus Christ.*

Immanuel, God with Us

> I heard a loud voice from the throne saying,
> "Now the dwelling of God is with men, and he will live with them.
> They will be his people, and God himself will be with them and be their God.
> He will wipe every tear from their eyes. There will be no more death or mourning
> or crying or pain, for the old order of things has passed away."

REVELATION 21:3-4

God came into human life as a man who shared our pain and sorrow. We remember how the Man of Sorrows was hurt with the horrible pain of crucifixion, but might he not have suffered the very physical pain of countless people besides? Who can say for certain what were the limits of the Lord's pain? In any case, he suffered doubly, for with his pain he also suffered an exquisite *consciousness* of all our pains and losses, and the consciousness was that of an infinite agapic love. In this way, he carried our sorrows with us, though he did not carry them all away.

The premise remains, of course, that this same Lord who carried our sorrows with us—and continues to carry them even now—will indeed some day take them away. In the vision of Revelation 21, the cure for sorrow is the presence of God-with-us: "he will wipe every tear from their eyes."

REFLECT: *What does the future promise of no more death or mourning or crying or pain mean to you? How can it shape your life today?*

The Arm of Humane Justice

"Love the Lord your God with all your heart and with all your soul
and with all your mind and with all your strength." . . .
"Love your neighbor as yourself." There is no commandment greater than these.

MARK 12:30-31

Love keeps the tattered edges of human culture from unraveling completely. It keeps the shaken foundational structures of civilization from crumbling. Love gives human society a future. Society exists when people are free participants in the wealth and responsibilities of the common life. Isolated from community, human existence is lonely, desperate and brutish. Apart from society we have no personal identity; apart from love we have no society.

Unless society is knit together with love, there is only efficient organization; and when efficiency is the highest value, persons are transformed into things whose value is their contribution to making things run. Without agapic love, efficiency can excuse anything; the weak, the voiceless, the unborn may all be sacrificed at the altar of efficiency.

Laws will not sustain a society, even though without law a society is lost. Laws need love. Love provides insight into people; it recognizes genuine differences between them—their needs and their circumstances. So love helps law to be fair and flexible—to be the arm of humane justice.

REFLECT: *Why did Jesus elevate loving the Lord our God and loving our neighbor above the making or keeping of laws?*

M O N D A Y

The Design of God's Love

Therefore, if anyone is in Christ, he is a new creation;
the old has gone, the new has come!

2 CORINTHIANS 5:17

God's love is too grand to be confined as a feeling within my soul. The design of God's love is large indeed. No nook or cranny of history is too small for its concern; no civilization too large for its power. In Christ, we are part of a movement of love that rolls on through time toward a new earth where all things will be right, where we all will be vitalized wholly by the love of God. Meanwhile, love carries the world along, "not wishing that any soul should perish, but that all should reach repentance" (see 2 Peter 3:9) and share in the experience of total healing, the time of the new creation.

REFLECT: *In what ways do you see God using you in his "movement of love that rolls on through time toward a new earth where all things will be right"?*

Overpowering Our Fears

*Then Mary took about a pint of pure nard, an expensive perfume;
she poured it on Jesus' feet and wiped his feet with her hair.
And the house was filled with the fragrance of the perfume.*

JOHN 12:3

There is a careless streak in love. It can be careless with goods, pouring out expensive perfume on a Master's feet and hair. A careful person would have measured it out beforehand—not too much (keeping some for oneself), not too little (ensuring that an impression of generosity is given). Love is also careless with one's self. It is risky to put oneself out for another, to go out of one's way to help another person—when one is not sure of how to do it well. One may be misunderstood, deceived or hurt. We could flub our overtures of love and end up looking ridiculous. Moved by love, however, we overpower our fear and take the risk.

PRAY: *Ask God to give you the courage to, like Mary, have a careless streak in your love of the Father and of your neighbor and yourself. Ask for the help to overpower your fear and take the risk.*

God's Unconditional Love

But I trust in your unfailing love; my heart rejoices in your salvation.

PSALM 13:5

Love can get us into trouble if we calculate costs. It can use our own money and time and energy and deprive of us our ego-pleasure. But in terms of what we *really* are, persons whom God loves *unconditionally*, we cannot lose by love's trust. We know that we are what we are because God has seen beneath the layers of dubious quality and ordinary sin and discerned in us persons worth redeeming. So when our love is betrayed, we have really lost nothing at all. What could we lose that is most deeply ours when all that we have is the product of God's love? One who is much loved owes much. One who loves much believes much.

REFLECT: *What makes it hard to trust in God's unconditional love for you?*

Checks and Balances

In you our fathers put their trust; they trusted and you delivered them.
They cried to you and were saved; in you they trusted and were not disappointed.

PSALM 22:4-5

We cannot live by Christian love alone. We also live by wisdom and intelligence. We are moved by justice. We are driven by eros. All of these will put checks and balances on love's readiness to believe. In our world, love needs such balances. But in the long run we are far better off trusting people too much than trusting too little. Being taken in now and then is a small price to pay—if it has to be paid—for not letting a neighbor down. Besides, trusting people is training for trusting God.

PRAY: *Read Psalm 22 as a prayer of supplication for the worries and fears you carry, and praise for the God in whom you've placed your trust.*

The Promise of Christ

> *We have this hope as an anchor for the soul, firm and secure.*
> *It enters the inner sanctuary behind the curtain, where Jesus, who went before us,*
> *has entered on our behalf. He has become a high priest forever, in the order of Melchizedek.*

HEBREWS 6:19

The promise of Christ is that *he* is our hope. This hope cannot fail because Christ will not and cannot fail. This is why Christian hope is often symbolized by an anchor, "a sure and steadfast anchor of the soul." Hope in Christian experience means: "I am *sure* as I face the future." Now we should note that this is true "because God's love has been poured into our hearts through the Holy Spirit" (see Romans 5:5). Love is the power behind the hope that "does not disappoint us." Love stimulates the certainty of Christian hope.

Hope looks to the promise of the final victory of Jesus Christ over all that hurts and kills. This is the hope that gives a person courage to praise today and to face tomorrow with expectancy even when one does not expect the problem to be solved. Love breeds this hope in both the person loved and the loving person.

REFLECT: *In what ways is Jesus like an anchor for you?*

Love Hopes All Things

Why are you downcast, O my soul? Why so disturbed within me?
Put your hope in God, for I will yet praise him, my Savior and my God

PSALM 43:5

Love is the power that blends desire and expectancy into hope. When love sees possibilities in the loved one, it recognizes these as created by God, whose love is the catalyst that can make all things new (2 Corinthians 5:17). Therefore, love *hopes* all things.

But we must not slide over the hard cases. Love often gives pain along with hope. This confronts us as one of the stern realities of a loving life. How can love keep a person hoping while relentless hammering of disappointments beats at his life? This is the cry of loving people in the clutches of personal pain.

But love hopes all things. The love that lets people be what they are—even when we desperately want them to be different from what they are—this love hopes all things. The paradox of love's power is that it sometimes gives new hope only as we let our fondest hopes die.

PRAY: *Ask the Lord for the ability to maintain hope in the midst of the relentless hammering of disappointments. Pray for the sure, strong anchor of Christ's love in the midst of the storms of life.*

MONDAY *Love Without Limits*

Love . . . always protects, always trusts, always hopes, always perseveres.

1 CORINTHIANS 13:4-7

Love hopes in a new way. This totally accepting love brings hope not for a miracle of healing but for the miracle of joy, which is the miracle of gratitude. This love brings hope that life is good, that it has point and meaning, and that the future ahead is one which we can walk into expectantly. In love we learn to *expect* to be surprised by God and joy—along with pain. Love is the power of a new hope that can coexist with pain.

Love hopes all things. How extravagant is Paul's song! How absurd, in the face of tough realities and expert prognoses, even to speak of such unlimited hope! But love, the power that suffers long without setting limits, is also the power that keeps hoping without setting due dates. Despair comes from deadlines set too early and hope defined too narrowly. Hope fails when love is a demand instead of a gift. Agapic love lets things and people be, and in the gift of letting things and people be, love becomes a power that creates a hope that will not disappoint us.

REFLECT: *Read all of 1 Corinthians 13 and reflect on the relationship between steadfast faith and hope in the Lord, and the ability to love others.*

*Everything that was written in the past was written to teach us,
so that through endurance and the encouragement of the Scriptures we might have hope.*

ROMANS 15:4

In biblical experience, endurance has a passive, accepting side called *patience*, and an active, aggressive side called *courage*. In patience we say Yes to life in the midst of evil assaults on our own existence. In courage we counterattack against the evil that assaults us. To endure is to blend patience and courage in the face of all that hurts us and so to grow into a fuller person.

We are dealing here with more than the mere power to *survive*. Even survival, admittedly, sometimes looks like more than we can manage. But being survivors only means we came through alive, that we managed to hang on, and St. Paul has much more in mind than hanging on. Enduring means growing and expanding as persons under pressure.

JOURNAL: *What are the things in your life that require patience and courage? Write down your thoughts, and in the weeks ahead revisit what you've written to see the ways God has helped you endure.*

The Bruises of Life

Those who hope in the LORD will renew their strength.
They will soar on wings like eagles;
they will run and not grow weary, they will walk and not be faint.

ISAIAH 40:31

When the Hebrew people were urged to keep waiting, they were always urged on to courage as well. "Wait for the LORD; be strong, and let your heart take courage; yea, wait for the LORD!" (Psalm 27:14 RSV).

People in the Christian age need to endure in virtually the same way as the Hebrews did. The bruises of life are still relentless, and the coming of God is deliberate and slow. The author of Hebrews speaks to the condition of many of us when he says, "You endured a hard struggle with sufferings" (Hebrews 10:32 RSV). The enduring is, of course, painful. Christ's own passion and cross is a model of Christian endurance, but his resurrection is a signal of victory through endurance. Salvation lies at the end of the tunnel: the one who endures to the end, said Jesus, will be saved (Matthew 10:22; 24:13).

REFLECT: *The passage from Isaiah 40 is a common one, but nevertheless one that brings great comfort to the heavy hearted. Why does the image of an eagle in flight convey such a sense of hope and strength?*

A New Commandment

A new command I give you: Love one another.
As I have loved you, so you must love one another.

JOHN 13:34

Love is a power that flows into persons and drives them to move toward others. Love enables people to do loving sorts of things and be loving sorts of persons. That love is a power explains why Paul personifies it, talking as if love itself did things. Love believes, he says. And love endures, hopes and bears all things. What he obviously means is that love is the power which enables people to endure, to believe and to hope. Knowing that love is a power can reduce the burden of love as a duty.

This is not to ignore the Christian *obligation* of love. Jesus called his disciples into the life of self-denying love when he said: "A new commandment I give to you, that you love one another; even as I have loved you." And this is only one of many declarations of the law of love. No question about it: love is a duty as well as a power. But the good news is that love is power. Love *enables* us to do what love obligates us to do.

REFLECT: *In what ways have you experienced God's love empowering you "to endure, to believe and to hope"?*

Feeling and Believing

> " 'If you can'?" said Jesus. "Everything is possible for him who believes."
> Immediately the boy's father exclaimed, "I do believe; help me overcome my unbelief!"

MARK 9:23-24

Faith does not break loose in my head with a whooping "Hurrah for God!" Believing sneaks into my soul while my mind is saying, "My God, where were you when I needed you?"

I am talking about real believing, the kind you do with your deepest self, down where your primeval feelings flow. The thinking part is not all that hard. I can think of arguments for God in my sleep. It is the feeling part that comes hard, the part that lets you know in the deep places of your soul that it is all right even when your head tells you everything is ghastly.

When I *feel* that I am loved while everything about me says I am unlovable, then I am believing, really believing. When I *feel* that life in this valley of death is much worth living, then I am believing. When I *feel* gratitude enough to make me glad, then I am believing. When I *feel* that all is right with me even when everything around me is the pits, then I am actually believing.

APPLY: *How do you handle the conflicts, when they arise, between what you think about God and what you feel in the midst of the tremors and questions and storms of life?*

The Surge of Honest Joy

The law was given through Moses; grace and truth came through Jesus Christ.

JOHN 1:17

Grace does come, this I know for sure.

Grace happens to me when I feel a surge of honest joy that makes me glad to be alive in spite of valid reasons for feeling terrible. Grace happens when I accept my wife's offer to begin again with me in love after I have hurt her. It happens when I feel powerfully free to follow my own conscience in spite of those who think I am either crazy or wicked. Grace is the gift of feeling sure that our future, even our dying, is going to turn out more splendidly than we dare imagine. Grace is the feeling of hope.

Yes, grace does happen. It happens on many layers of my life. But one thing is the same all the way through. Grace makes me feel that it's all right even when everything is all wrong.

JOURNAL: *Take time to journal your own list of evidences of grace in your life.*

MONDAY *Grace Be with You*

> *May the grace of the Lord Jesus Christ, and the love of God,*
> *and the fellowship of the Holy Spirit be with you all.*

2 CORINTHIANS 13:14

The word *grace* has often been no more than a mere commonplace pleasantry. Saint Paul picked up the old bromide from a trivial custom of his time, and closed all of his letters with a variation on the "grace" theme: "Grace be with you," he said, or something similar. What a cliché! You could have heard it everywhere Greek was spoken in those days. A man lifted a glass of wine to a stranger he met at a bar and said, "Here's grace to you!" He signed off a letter to a person he despised, "Grace be with you." A stale, flip, silly little lie people used to oil the machinery of trivial conversation. A commonplace, nothing more.

But now, Saint Paul rescued this anemic commonplace, dipped it into a whole new reality, and made it a signal of God's assurance that *life can be all right just when everything in it is all wrong.* The reality of Jesus transformed the cliché of grace into the reality of God, coming into our time, our history, our lives to make things right at the center.

REFLECT: *How has your Christian journey transformed the notion of grace from simply a cliché into something deeper and more abiding?*

The First Face of Grace

*Just as sin reigned in death, so also grace might reign through righteousness
to bring eternal life through Jesus Christ our Lord.*

ROMANS 5:21

This is one amazing thing about grace, its surprising contradiction of the tender conscience. Conscience condemns; grace contradicts its condemnation. Conscience says, It's all wrong because you are wrong. Grace says, It's all right even if you are wrong. Grace is always a surprise. It is not surprising that God wants us to be honest, fair, decent and kind. Every deity conceived in the pious imaginations of religious folk wants these things. But the surprising word of the amazing God of Jesus Christ, the word coming from the cross where he died to make it right, the good word to a sinful soul, is this word: it is all right, at the very core of life, all right, precisely when we are in the wrong. This is pardon, the first face of grace that embraces us.

PRAY: *Thank God for the pardon you have received in Christ, the first face of grace that embraces us.*

The Pardoning of Grace

With great power the apostles continued to testify to the resurrection of the Lord Jesus, and much grace was upon them all.

ACTS 4:33

Grace, in its second face, is the power to lead you closer to his image and make you a better person today than you were yesterday. But we will not sense how amazing this power is unless we see that it is unlike any energy we manipulate through our technology. Grace is a power totally unlike any we create in nuclear reactors; it is different from all physical force. But it is different, too, from moral force; grace does not make us better people by bullying us into moral improvement. The power to make us better works when God freely persuades us that it is all right with us the way we are. The power of grace is paradoxical.

When you are freed by the pardoning of grace, you are most powerful. When you feel sure that you can never be condemned for what you are, that no judgment, no catastrophic guilt can hurt you, the power begins to work! When grace persuades you it is all right with you even when you are wrong, then the power begins to work to make you right.

PRAY: *Thank God for the second face of grace—the power of the Spirit to lead you closer to the kind of life modeled by Jesus.*

The Amazing Promise

Since we have been justified through faith, we have peace with God through
our Lord Jesus Christ, through whom we have gained access by faith into this grace
in which we now stand. And we rejoice in the hope of the glory of God.

ROMANS 5:1-2

Grace is the power to live now as if things are going to be all right tomorrow—the third face of grace. The power, mind you, is not born from a desperate gambler's hunch, against long odds, that things are bound to get better. It is a power generated by the Spirit of Jesus, who has convincing evidence that God has a way of leading us through disaster into victory and making promises come true. Grace is a mysterious power to live as if you know tomorrow will be better than today, even though common sense gives you odds that tomorrow will be the pits.

When common sense says that life is frozen in a block of despair, when the pundits say there is no answer, when even theologians tell you that God has abandoned you to your fate . . . may grace be to you, as the amazing promise that your future is open to God's surprising will for your good.

PRAY: *Offer a prayer of thanks for the promise that God will lead us through the challenge of life into victory, for the grace that is a mysterious power to believe that tomorrow will be better than today.*

Being a Better Person

Stand firm and hold to the teachings we passed on to you,
whether by word of mouth or by letter. May our Lord Jesus Christ himself and God our Father,
who loved us and by his grace gave us eternal encouragement and good hope,
encourage your hearts and strengthen you in every good deed and word.

2 THESSALONIANS 2:15-17

Why do we call grace amazing? Grace is amazing because it works against the grain of common sense. Hard-nosed common sense will tell you that you are too wrong to meet the standards of a holy God; pardoning grace tells you that it's all right in spite of so much in you that is wrong. Realistic common sense tells you that you are too weak, too harassed, too human to change for the better; grace gives you power to send you on the way to being a better person. Plain common sense may tell you that you are caught in a rut of fate or futility; grace promises that you can trust God to have a better tomorrow for you than the day you have made for yourself.

APPLY: *Which face of God's grace do you most need to seek today?*

The Miracle of Forgiveness

In him we have redemption through his blood, the forgiveness of sins,
in accordance with the riches of God's grace

EPHESIANS 1:7

Forgiveness, at bottom, is a very simple sort of miracle. Forgiveness is a new beginning. Forgiveness is starting over and trying it again with the person who caused you pain. Take God, for instance. When God forgives, he offers us a new start with him. He holds out his hand and says, "Come on, take it, I want to be your friend again. In spite of everything, I want to be with you, and I want to be under you and over you and in you, as the loving power of your existence. I am not going to let anything you do get in my way. So let's begin again." This is what God does when he forgives: he breaks down the walls we build and gets into the back yard of our souls to make a new relationship.

PRAY: *Turn this devotional selection into a prayer of thanksgiving that God wants to be our friend, that he has broken down the walls that separated us.*

MONDAY *A Parable of Joy*

Praise be to the God and Father of our Lord Jesus Christ,
who has blessed us in the heavenly realms with every spiritual blessing in Christ.

EPHESIANS 1:3

What is joy? I suspect that, to answer this question, each of us has to locate a moment in his or her own life, a moment of special joy, seize hold of it, examine it, and let it be a parable of joy.

My own joy parable came one night after hearing a concert by Isaac Stern and the Los Angeles Philharmonic. He played one of the romantic concertos that set my heart on fire, and I was deeply moved. So were we all. We heard him. We received his gift, and when he was finished, we blessed him. We gave him the hallowed benedictions of our sweet applause. He took joy in our blessing, and he kept coming back for more. And when he came back, we took to our feet. We were swept away, beside ourselves with gratitude, and I suddenly realized that I was enjoying the applause more than I had enjoyed the concert. And I knew why.

In the receiving of Stern's gift, and in the giving of our blessing, we were enacting a parable of the meaning of life under God in this universe. We had received a truly great gift. In turn, we were moved by the feelings of gratitude for the gift and a desire to bless the giver.

APPLY: *Locate a moment when you were in touch with "special joy." What were the circumstances? What made it special? Offer a prayer of thanksgiving for this story of joy.*

Glorifying God

This day is sacred to our Lord.
Do not grieve, for the joy of the LORD is your strength.

NEHEMIAH 8:10

You and I were created for joy, and if we miss it, we miss the reason for our existence! Moreover, the reason Jesus Christ lived and died on earth was to restore us to the joy we have lost. Jesus himself told us: all that he said to us on earth came down to one primary goal, that we should share his joy. The church officially echoed Jesus when it taught us that the chief end of men and women was to glorify God and enjoy him forever. C. S. Lewis sensed it when he remarked that joy is the chief business of heaven (and, I would add, of earth as well). So we can safely believe that when we think about joy we are at the edge of life's deepest secret. We are not talking about emotional frills and psychic indulgences; we are talking about the discovery of all-rightness in the essence of life.

JOURNAL: *How can you deal with the things that rob you of joy and more fully live at the edge of life's deepest secret: joy in the essence of life?*

This Is the Day!

This is the day that the Lord has made; let us rejoice and be glad in it.

PSALM 118:24

Joy is our inheritance, our birthright. It is for us only to let the Spirit open our lives to joy; we do not need to earn it. Do you doubt your right to be joyful? Then listen to the Word again. God has made your day, this day, and he has given you the right to receive it with gratitude.

This is the day! Take it first in its simple, literal sense. Today, that square on your calendar that marks out another block of time on earth. Today, not tomorrow, not some dreamed-of-future when you can get out of the rat race for good, when you are in the 50-percent tax bracket, and you finally fulfill yourself in a new career. Not a day in a memory's glow, not a day in fantasy's vision, but this day, here, now, whatever its pains or problems or punishment. This is the day! God made it, set you in it, and joy in it is your inalienable right.

REFLECT: *If joy is our inheritance, our birthright, why do we often experience so little of it? How do we recover it? Hear the word of the Lord once again: "This is the day the Lord has made; let us rejoice and be glad in it"!*

Joy's Integrity

And we pray this in order that you may . . . have great endurance and patience, . . .
joyfully giving thanks to the Father, who has qualified you to share
in the inheritance of the saints in the kingdom of light.

COLOSSIANS 1:10-12

If our joy is honest joy, it must somehow be congruous with human tragedy. This is the test of joy's integrity: is it compatible with pain? Or is joy the cheap charade of a superficial society of lotus eaters?

Only the heart that hurts has the right to joy. Only the person who cries for the needless death of children has the right to bless God for the gift of life. You truly celebrate the gift of your existence only when you also cry out in pain for people whose existence is the constant humiliation of human injustice. You can shake your tambourine, you can speak in the ecstatic frenzy of a thousand charismatic tongues, but your noise is only self-indulgent gibberish unless your joy is tempered by the miseries of God's people around the world.

REFLECT: *How do you respond to the hurt of those who experience injustice in the world, while still clinging to the joy that is yours?*

Grace and Confession

> *If we confess our sins, he is faithful and just and will forgive us our sins*
> *and purify us from all unrighteousness.*
>
> 1   J O H N   1 : 9

In Thomas Hardy's classic *Tess of the D'Urbervilles*, Tess is a young bride who gambles her happiness, her very future, on her new husband's power to be gracious. She risks everything by telling him, on her wedding night, about a tragic mistake in her past relationship with another man. As she confesses, his body stiffens, his lips become tight, his dry eyes freeze in a blank stare. She gambled on his love and lost, and her life was over. Confession is a gamble on grace.

A confession includes acknowledgment of your own responsibility, the experience of shared pain and a readiness to gamble on grace. With these, any confession can be the beginning of a miracle that tears down a wall that alienates you and can build a bridge you can walk across to each other's forgiveness.

R E F L E C T : *In what ways is confession an act of "readiness to gamble on grace"? How do you incorporate confession in your own spiritual practices?*

A New Beginning

Be kind and compassionate to one another, forgiving each other,
just as in Christ God forgave you.

EPHESIANS 4:32

The miracle of forgiving is the creation of a new beginning. It does not always take away the hurt. It does not deny the past injury. It merely refuses to let them stand in the way of a new start. You do not have to understand why he did it. You do not have to get the whole story straight, to sew all the loose ends together so you can be sure there are no secrets left. You certainly do not have to squeeze every ounce of guilt from the soul of the person who did you wrong. You just begin where you are in your shared pain. You both hurt, and so you make your shared pain the starting line of a new relationship.

And you walk together into the future. What future? Who knows? All you have is a new beginning; no guarantee of where it will end. The future is going to bring more pain, you can be sure of that much. More confession, more shared pain with people who hurt you. More new beginnings. We never stand still.

REFLECT: *The miracle of forgiving does not always take away the hurt, the passage says. But it does help us on our way to a new start. How have you seen this evident in your own life?*

MONDAY *Gracious Living*

> *It is a very small thing that I should be judged by you or by any human court.*
> *I do not even judge myself. . . . It is the Lord who judges me.*

1 CORINTHIANS 4:3-4 NRSV

One of the fine arts of gracious living is the art of living freely with our critics. When we have the grace to be free in the presence of those who judge our lives and evaluate our actions, we have Christian freedom. And, feeling free, we feel as if things cannot be all wrong.

We will always have critics, of course. There is no escaping criticism. Critics are all around us: some welcomed, some self-appointed nuisances. They size us up, take our measure, weigh us in their scales and form their own opinions about our lives. They may approve of us. They may think we are walking disasters. They may think we are too conservative, too liberal, too easygoing, too serious, too wicked, too saintly. They may be right or, on the other hand, they may be wrong. But they will criticize; they will call us to account before the bar of *their* judgment.

PRAY: *Ask God to help you live freely and lightly with your critics.*

Finding Us Faithful

*The fruit of the Spirit is love, joy, peace, patience, kindness, goodness, faithfulness,
gentleness and self-control. Against such things there is no law.*

GALATIANS 5:22-23

What God expects of us, says Saint Paul, is that we be faithful. He puts us on earth as caretakers (or stewards, in older English). He put each of us here to take care of something. And what he asks of us is that we be faithful in taking care of it. There is something in life for each of us to care for. He does not ask that we be flawless, only faithful; not fantastic, not fabulous, only faithful. Being faithful means finding out what you are here to take care of and then giving it your best shot. And God is your critic. If you have trouble living with this critic, know this: grace can set you free in the presence even of your divine critic.

JOURNAL: *Write down your thoughts in response to the question, "In the light of God's call on my life, what am I on earth to take care of?"*

Opening Doors to Wonder

*Do not forget to entertain strangers, for by so doing some people
have entertained angels without knowing it.*

HEBREWS 13:2

Amazing grace, how sweet the sound that saved a wretch like me"; let that
old song settle in your heart and you can never close your heart's door to wonder again.

Keep a door open to wonder and even the ordinary people around you will
take on an odd dimension of mystery. Every person you know will be a potential eye-opener. You may meet people you do not like, but you will never again
meet a person you can take for granted. Wonder kills stereotypes. All the people clustered around you—people bound to you by routine loyalty, others
floating at the fringes of your inner circle—they are all awesome folk, each one
hiding a mystery far too deep for the likes of you to have all figured out.

APPLY: *Select a book, such as Arthur Gordon's* Wonder: Moments that Keep
You Falling in Love with Life, *to help you be more attuned to a sense of wonder in
your day-to-day, ordinary existence.*

THURSDAY *Unraveling the Mystery*

I have been crucified with Christ and I no longer live, but Christ lives in me.
The life I live in the body, I live by faith in the Son of God,
who loved me and gave himself for me.

GALATIANS 2:20

If we could get tuned to the wonder in other people, we may also be ready for the mystery of our own selves. There is more to me than meets my eye and more to you than meets yours. You have not even begun to unravel the mystery of your self and your mind; you are deep, unfathomably deep. You cannot be a shallow person; God does not make shallow people. You can, if you choose, close your own mind to the depths within you. But you cannot be shallow.

This is ten thousand times clearer if you are a Christian. Consider this wondrous self-discovery. Can you see yourself this way and still suppose that you could be a shallow, predictable person: "I live, yet not I, but Christ lives in me." There is the mind-boggling truth about you: Jesus Christ, in his Spirit, present in you, without shoving the real you aside, at the depths of your existence.

REFLECT: *Reflect on the truth that the Spirit of Christ lives and dwells within you. What does that say about the love and grace of God? How do you respond to this wonderful gift?*

Open to Wonder

> *They recognized him as the same man who used to sit*
> *begging at the temple gate called Beautiful, and they were*
> *filled with wonder and amazement at what had happened to him.*

A C T S   3 : 1 0

It takes grace in our time to keep our minds open to wonder, to be ready for the tug from God, the push from the Spirit, and the revelation of deep things from the hearts of ordinary people. It takes grace, but it is a great gift. If you have a place in your life where your eyes can still gape, your knees quiver and your mind boggles, you are open to wonder. And, open to wonder, you are ready for God's surprises, even the greatest of all; that it can be all right when everything is wrong.

You may be able, when the dark sky falls upon you, when life is skewed, your situation off center, you may just be able to see what others cannot see, at a level below any they guess existed. In spite of everything, you may be able to know that you are all right inside the hands of an invisible but wonderful God. You will miss this saving sense if your heart is closed to wonder. So let there be wonder in your life! Blessed are the wonder-full, for they shall see God, and they alone shall know themselves.

JOURNAL: *Where are the places in your life where your "eyes still gape, your knees quiver and your mind boggles"?*

Suffering with Christ

We are children of God, and if children, then heirs, heirs of God
and joint heirs with Christ—if, in fact, we suffer with him.

ROMANS 8:16-17 NRSV

A friend talked to me not long ago about an unusual worry simmering on the back burners of his conscience. Life was treating him well. He had a lovely wife and a pretty good marriage. He was in good shape, strong as a healthy ox. All his children were beautiful, talented and doing well. He had won star status in his field of work. So what was he worried about? He was worried that something might be wrong if everything was this good.

I should tell you that he was a Christian too, and knew that Jesus led his followers to expect things to go wrong sometimes as a consequence of their commitment. But he had not suffered, not much anyway. Where did that leave him? Was there a soft spot in the underbelly of his Christian commitment?

About the same time, I was jolted by what must be the Bible's toughest word on suffering. It goes like this: we are children of God—along with Jesus—*if, in fact,* we suffer with him. It is the small print in a footnote of the gospel: only sufferers need apply. There is no heaven for us unless we suffer with him on earth. Maybe my friend does well to worry.

REFLECT: *What do you make of the passage from Romans 8? In what ways, if any, can you identify with having "suffered with him" on earth?*

MONDAY *A Suffering Savior*

> *Just as the sufferings of Christ flow over into our lives,*
> *so also through Christ our comfort overflows.*
>
> 2 CORINTHIANS 1:5

It must be transparent to anyone who knows the life of Jesus that he was a genius at suffering with people. Suffering *with* is what was wholly unique about how Jesus suffered on earth. He certainly suffered a lot, and he certainly suffered *from* the hands of other people. He suffered from the rage of frightened bigots. He suffered from the cool cruelty of imperious Rome. He suffered from the facile fade-outs of his friends. He suffered from hard nails in his soft skin. And yet, he did not suffer uniquely as the Savior of the world because he suffered a lot. There have been other great sufferers besides Jesus.

What was special about Jesus' suffering was not the quantity, but the quality, not how much he suffered from others, but how he suffered with others. It was suffering *with* sufferers that made him a Savior.

REFLECT: *Scan passages of Scripture that speak of Christ's suffering, such as Romans 8:17, Philippians 3:10 and 1 Peter 1:33. Meditate on both the quantity and the quality of his sufferings on our behalf.*

The Least of These

The righteous will answer him, "Lord, when did we see you?" . . .
The King will reply, "I tell you the truth, whatever you did for
one of the least of these brothers of mine, you did for me."

MATTHEW 25:37-40

If you want to know who the vicar of Christ is, find yourself a hurting human being in your neighborhood. Jesus is found where people are putting up with things they want to go away, trying to cope when everything is all wrong. He is represented on earth by the wounded. He is not among them as a visitor, not even as a comforting friend. He is one of them; he is any or all of them. Talk about transference of one's identity; in his mind, Jesus becomes the human sufferer.

Jesus points to suffering people and says, "There I am." He says it because he feels it. He feels their hurt and, in the sharing of pain, equates the sufferer with himself. Jesus *is* your hurting neighbor. He *is* the hurting child. He *is* your hurting enemy. He is anyone who is *from* anything not of his or her own choosing. If you feel the hurt of any person who hurts, you are suffering with Jesus.

PRAY: *Ask God to help you discern and respond to the hurt or need of another person and to respond, as Jesus would, through the power of his Spirit.*

Feeling Another's Hurt

Dear friends, let us love one another, for love comes from God.
Everyone who loves has been born of God and knows God.

1 J O H N 4 : 7

Where do we get the power to feel another person's hurt, keep feeling it for a long time, no relief in sight, when we have enough pains of our own? We need more love than we have. But God is love. So we need God. Why deny it? We need God if we want to move beyond our own tiredness and clumsiness, move into the life of another, not to get pleasure from her but to take her pain into us. And there, I've said it all. If we cannot do it without God, it means we do it with God if we do it at all. So when we do suffer with someone else, even a little, we may be sure we are moving on the wave of God. We are doing what God does.

JOURNAL: *"We need God if we want to move beyond our own tiredness and clumsiness, move into the life of another." Journal your thoughts in response to this statement, asking God to help you make that move.*

Earthen Vessels

We have this treasure in jars of clay,
to show that this all-surpassing power comes from God and not from us.

2 CORINTHIANS 4:7 NRSV

We have this treasure in earthen vessels. We are the vessels, of course, each of us individually and together—common lumps of clay carrying the greatest gift ever given to the human family. God packages and distributes his divine gift in ordinary, very undivine humanity, so that we will not admire the wrapping so much that we discount the gift.

We are the vessels; what is the treasure?

Saint Paul tells us that the treasure is "the knowledge of the glory of God in the face of Jesus Christ." The knowledge is always a knowledge of experience; it is not a head-trip, though it certainly includes the mind. But to know God is to experience him, to live with him, to be loved by him and to love him. To experience the *glory* of God is to experience God's excellence, his splendid essence; it is to know the secret of what God is really like.

REFLECT: *How have you taken steps to "know the secret of what God is really like"? What has been the role of Scripture? your church tradition? solitude and silence and other spiritual disciplines? your church community? prayer?*

The Face of Jesus

Anyone who has seen me has seen the Father.

JOHN 14:9 NEB

If you want to experience what God is really like, if you want to know his glory, you see it in the face of a man. His name is Jesus.

The face of Jesus? We must think of more than the image he could see in a pool of water, more than the cheeks down which a tear could run, more than clear Jewish eyes that never flinched in fear or shame. The face of Jesus is the living profile of a human being at work among the people who needed and cared for him. The face of Jesus means all that he was to people, all that he said, all that he did. The life of Jesus, in totality, or in detail, the tears of sadness, the sighs of weakness, the miracles of power, the words of truth—this is the face of Jesus.

APPLY: *How would you describe the "face of Jesus" that you see in your mind's eye? Select a book such as Frederick Buechner's* The Faces of Jesus *to expand your reflection on this meditation.*

The Glory of God

All this took place to fulfill what the Lord had said through the prophet:
"The virgin will be with child and will give birth to a son, and they will call him Immanuel"—
which means, "God with us."

MATTHEW 1:22-23

In the birth of Jesus, we see God coming in weak and vulnerable human form. God chooses to share our location and condition. God *is with us*. In the death of Jesus, we see God present in suffering human form. God chooses to take our part instead of being our enemy. *God is for us*. In the resurrection and ascension, we see God in victorious human form. In this form, insinuating himself into the depths of our very being, God *is in us*—as the Spirit of Christ. Three views of Jesus, three views of God.

Here, then, in a cameo, is the glory of God. Here is what God is really like. He is the God who is with us, the God who is for us and the God who is in us.

JOURNAL: *Reflect on this trilogy of perspectives on the reality of Christ in the life of the believer—God is with us. God is for us. God is in us.*

M O N D A Y

God's Kind of Clay Pot

Does not the potter have the right to make out of the same lump of clay
some pottery for noble purposes and some for common use?

ROMANS 9:21

The earliest heresy in the Christian church happened when people denied that Jesus was a real human being. The same heresy gets into our heads when we hear that God might show his grace through our faces. We like to suppose that if we really did have God's treasure in us, we would be able to fly, swoop in from anywhere to rescue our children, rescue our friends and win the heart of any Lois Lane. Fumbling old Clark Kents that most of us are, we bleed, we hurt, we can hardly cope, let alone rescue a threatened city. It is hard to believe—but God's way is to put his treasure in the Clark Kents of the world and not in supermen. So stop dreaming; you aren't going to be Superman, you're just an earthen vessel. But you are God's kind of clay pot.

REFLECT: *Is it hard for you to believe that God uses a "Clark Kent" or "Lois Lane" like you to be the face of grace to the world? How can you embrace the reality that you are God's kind of clay pot?*

Being the Hand and Heart

They will lay up treasure for themselves as a firm foundation for the coming age,
so that they may take hold of the life that is truly life.

1 TIMOTHY 6:19

Keep in touch with yourself as the fragile, fallible but functional and fillable piece of ordinary humanity that you are. Keep in touch with yourself because, just as you are, you are qualified to hold and to share the treasure of God. Walk into the unknown possibilities of tomorrow with your human weakness; carry with you the blemishes of your soul and the commonness of your spirit. Just be the earthen vessel that you are. Let God fill you, and then you may be the hand and the heart, as well as the face of God, to someone who needs him more than he needs anything else in the world. When it happens to you, you will know for sure that, no matter how wrong everything around you is, there is something most magnificently right with you.

PRAY: *Ask God to fill you so that you may be the hand, the heart and the face of God to someone in need today.*

The Invisible Hand of God

Ask and it will be given to you; seek and you will find;
knock and the door will be opened to you. For everyone who asks receives;
he who seeks finds; and to him who knocks, the door will be opened.

MATTHEW 7:7-8

It is a quirk in ordinary people that they keep the door closed to the gracious gift of being all right when everything is all wrong. Down at the bottom, where feelings get too fierce for us to face, down where we press our anger into knots too tight to untie, we shut the door and keep it locked until God's invisible hand silently spins off the combination and gets through the door of pain and tiredness with the reality of Christ's grace. Ordinary people are people who have to struggle to make it and, in the struggle, turn away the gift that can enable them, not merely to make it, but to be very glad for the gift of trying.

JOURNAL: *What blocks you from access to the gift of God's grace? Ask God to open your eyes to the reality of Christ's grace.*

Bridging the Gap

For if, when we were God's enemies, we were reconciled to him through the death of his Son,
how much more, having been reconciled, shall we be saved through his life!
Not only is this so, but we also rejoice in God through our Lord Jesus Christ,
through whom we have now received reconciliation.

ROMANS 5:10-12

The mystery is that God was in Jesus Christ reconciling the world to himself. When Jesus lived as a man on our native soil, living as a person who gave his life for others, dying and living again, he was about the business of making it right for us at the core of life. He let it be known to all, once and for all, that when we are confronted by the God who made us and holds us in his hands, we are facing a God who loves us and wants our good.

He built a bridge over the great gap that separated us from a holy God; the bridge he built was the cross where he was crucified. Since the cross of Christ, God and the world are reconciled, friends once again, with God bent on turning the world, and our lives in it, into a thing of beauty and justice and glory.

PRAY: *Ask God to continue to turn your life into a thing of beauty and justice and glory—and, in doing so, that Christ would be glorified.*

The Secret of Grace

May he strengthen your hearts so that you will be blameless and holy
in the presence of our God and Father
when our Lord Jesus comes with all his holy ones.

1 THESSALONIANS 3:13

At the center, where life is open to the Creator and Savior God, we are held, led, loved, cared for and inseparably bound into the future that he has for every child whom he claims as his.

The important thing is that an extraordinary gift is available to ordinary people. It is the gift of an open door, the rusty hinged door of angry, hurting, tired hearts, an open door for a grace that restores us to truth, the truth that, at the depths, between ordinary people and God, it is all right and always will be.

REFLECT: *In times when it appears that everything around the edges of your life appears to be all wrong, what helps you maintain the belief that at life's core it is all right?*

God's Compassionate Patience

Suffering produces perseverance; perseverance, character; and character, hope.
And hope does not disappoint us, because God has poured out
his love into our hearts by the Holy Spirit, whom he has given us.

ROMANS 5:3-5

God's compassionate patience is the answer to our personal impatience. From the control center of our worried lives, God's patience often looks like cold indifference. He takes so awfully long that he does not seem to care. But he has a lot of time and, like an artist who loves his work, he will not be rushed. Nor should we be rushed, especially when it comes to closing down, terminating, giving up on the nasty problems we want solved now. We should not give up too quickly on our troubled marriages. We should not give up too quickly on our troubled children. We should not give up too quickly on our troubled selves. Don't demand that everything be all right today. Give God time, as he gives us time.

APPLY: *Study Psalm 120, 124 or 126 and reflect on the themes of obedience and perseverance. Eugene Peterson's Bible study* Perseverance: A Long Obedience in the Same Direction *is one means of learning to pray and wait patiently in the midst of what seems like God's cold indifference.*

M O N D A Y   *God Gives Us a Choice*

Should I not be concerned about Nineveh, that great city?

JONAH 4:11 NRSV

God gives us grace to imitate his patience. He gives us a choice. Will we be the Jonahs of the world who demand instant and violent solutions to our problems? Or will we let God take his time, and let him show us, in his way, that we do not have to foreclose on the future, let him show us that it can get to be all right tomorrow even though everything seems incredibly wrong today. When he does, he will make it feel all right *with us* beginning today, even if we have to wait for the rest.

PRAY: *Ask God for the grace to imitate his patience—with others, with ourselves and as we wait to see the answers to the cries of our hearts.*

Modeling Life in Heaven

Once again men and women of ripe old age will sit in the streets of Jerusalem,
each with cane in hand because of his age.
The city streets will be filled with boys and girls playing there.

ZECHARIAH 8:4-5

The gift of hope makes every person, as well as the whole family of humanity, very valuable; the vision of future rightness sends back a stamp of rightness into the present. It also makes life a little more playful. What we cannot do in a million calendar squares, God will do in his own time. So the new world will not be lost if we play a little on our way. Besides, when we play we are modeling life in heaven.

REFLECT: *What are your images of heaven? Do you envision a place where laughter and play and lightheartedness reside? Or are your images more serious in nature? Reread the description of Jerusalem from Zechariah. Might this be an apt description of our heavenly home?*

Community and Christian Hope

Let justice roll on like a river, righteousness like a never-failing stream!

AMOS 5:24

I hope, with human hope, that my community will be a fair place for people to live, a place where people help each other, care for each other, and where all people have both enough to eat and someone to love them. But I doubt that I will ever find such a perfect community. I hope, with Christian hope, that we will all love each other with a love that finds its highest pleasure when other people have what is rightly theirs, capped with inexpressible joys. And my sure hope for a community of perfect love and perfect justice makes my present human family worth saving and healing.

REFLECT: *Where does "Christian hope" originate, and how is it nurtured in the life of the believer? What are the ways in which Christian hope and community are being offered to others where you worship?*

The Virtue of Imperfection

So then, just as you received Christ Jesus as Lord, continue to live in him,
rooted and built up in him, strengthened in the faith as you were taught,
and overflowing with thankfulness.

COLOSSIANS 2:6-7

A friend of mine tells his wife that she is a model of perfect imperfection. He has a fine sense for the virtue of imperfection.

Imperfection is the mark of a good person who is capable of being even better. To feel our imperfection is to feel the energy of our potential—the push from what we are toward what we have it in us to be. Imperfection is not the wage of sin; it is the gift of our finitude, as being a bud before becoming a flower is the gift of nature's leisure.

Grace-based people live lightly with their imperfections because they see their imperfections as reason to be grateful and thankful to be limited creatures with unlimited potential.

REFLECT: *Are you able to "live lightly with your imperfections"? Are you able to view imperfection as a virtue, pointing us to our potential to become something more than we are?*

Our Ultimate Assurance

Then you will know the truth, and the truth will set you free.

JOHN 8:32

Shame and grace are the two counterforces in the human spirit; shame depresses; grace lifts. Shame is like gravity, a psychic force that pulls us down. Grace is like levitation, a spiritual force that defies gravity. If our spiritual experience does not lighten our life, we are not experiencing grace.

Grace is our ultimate assurance that our false self has no validity and its message of shame has no threat. We can disclaim it with one sentence: I am accepted by grace. We can reject it. We can refuse to listen to it. We can cleanse ourselves from its influence forever.

Unhealthy shame is like a hard shell that we need to crack in order to find the beauty within us. It also keeps us from owning the shadowy and ugly things inside of us. Grace gives us courage to pry open the shell and look at both the beauty and the beast within.

REFLECT: *How have you experienced the heaviness of unhealthy shame? How has the grace of God been a counterforce in the midst of that shame? Pray for the boldness to disclaim shame by saying, "I am accepted by grace."*

The Lightest Feeling of Life

Anyone who trusts in him will never be put to shame.

ROMANS 10:11

The lightness of grace does not lift all the sandbags that drag the spirit down. It lightens life by removing one very dead weight in particular—the weight of anxiety about being an unacceptable person. It extracts the internal threat of healthy shame. It gives us courage to track down the sources of unhealthy shame, see it for the undeserved pain it is and take steps to purge our lives of it completely. It sets loose the lightest feeling of life: being accepted—totally, unreservedly accepted.

PRAY: *Pray for the ability to overcome your anxieties and lean into the lightness of God's grace.*

MONDAY

The Maker of the Universe

*All have sinned and fall short of the glory of God,
and are justified freely by his grace through the redemption that came by Christ Jesus.*

ROMANS 3:23-24

Grace is too unpredictable, too lavish, too delicious for us to stay sober about it. What can you do with such unchecked generosity but smack your lips, slosh it around your tongue and savor it with joy?

I taste grace when a friend, for no reason at all, tells me that she loves me. I see it when my left leg goes where I tell it to go. I feel it when I take a deep breath of smog-free air. I savor it when the woman I have loved for forty years murmurs, strokes me and makes me to move over to my side of the bed and give her some room to curl up beside me.

I savor it most happily when I accept the fact that I am accepted as I am, with my ogres, my demons and my angels, my blundered past, my frail virtues, all mixed together, undeserving and yet worthy at the same time, accepted by the Maker and Keeper of the universe.

PRAY: *Thank God for his acceptance of you even with your own ogres, blundered past, frail virtues and everything else all mixed together.*

The Clarity of the Gospel

This is love: not that we loved God, but that he loved us
and sent his Son as an atoning sacrifice for our sins.

1 JOHN 4:10

God must have wanted to create a world for the same reason that he wanted to redeem it. The gospel tells us very clearly why he wanted to redeem the world: God sent his Son not to condemn the world but to save it. And he wanted to save it for one simple reason: he loved it. Now, if love is why he wants to fix the world, love must be the reason he made it in the first place.

Mind, now, I am sure that God is thrilled when anyone looks at the "purple mountain majesty" of our earth and breaks out with a "Glory be to God." And thrilled too when a saved sinner lifts his hands and sings "Amazing Grace." But it seems to me that we make God out to be an absolute narcissist—someone who loves only himself—when we say that his main motive for creating the world was to get glory and honor for himself. It simply must be that he created us in order to love us, all of us, and all of us with the same love.

P R A Y : *Personalize the Scripture passage above and turn it into a prayer, acknowledging that God sent his only Son because he loved you; he sent his Son as an atoning sacrifice for your sins.*

No Inferior Grace

> *The grace of God has appeared that offers salvation to all people.*
> *It teaches us to say "No" to ungodliness and worldly passions,*
> *and to live self-controlled, upright and godly lives in this present age.*

TITUS 2:11-12 TNIV

There is no such thing, it seems to me now, as a second-class, or common, grace. God's grace can never be common, never second-rate. It is always special. Always amazing. I now believe that the whole idea of an inferior grace for reprobates was something dreamed up to make the doctrine of reprobation seem a mite less horrible than it is. If we stop insulting God by ascribing such a dark doctrine to him, we will have no need of any "common grace." We will have only the one marvelous grace of God for all humankind. What all this comes down to is this: The most glorious thing about God is that he made us not so that we could give him glory, but that he could give us love. And that great love leads him to be gracious to all.

REFLECT: *"The most glorious thing about God is that he made us not so that we could give him glory, but that he could give us love." How do you respond to this assertion?*

A Long Obedience

> *For just as through the disobedience of the one man the many were made sinners,*
> *so also through the obedience of the one man the many will be made righteous.*

ROMANS 5:19

With God, we are called to act not in self-interest but in obedience to his moral law. The fact, however, is that obeying his moral law leads us to what is in the best interests of all of us. A rational God who would go to the trouble of creating a world full of free-willed people must, I thought, have a design in mind for how these people could best live together. God's design is what makes things right or wrong. We do right if we live according to his design. We do wrong when we violate his design. So what we call moral law—or the divine commandments—is a manual for life at its best.

REFLECT: *What is God's design for how we best live together as a human race? Read Exodus 20 as a starting point for understanding God's design.*

F R I D A Y *A Good Moral Life*

> *You shall not give false testimony against your neighbor.*
> *You shall not covet your neighbor's house.*
> *You shall not covet your neighbor's wife, or his manservant or maidservant,*
> *his ox or donkey, or anything that belongs to your neighbor.*

E X O D U S   2 0 : 1 6 - 1 7

Much of the time, if our hearts are pure, the commandments are all we need to live a good moral life. We know that when we talk, we must be truthful. When we make a promise, we must keep it. When we want something our neighbor has, we must keep our hands off of it. When our neighbor does us wrong, we must not kill him for revenge. And no matter how unhappy our marriages may be, we must be faithful to them. Thus, for most of our daily moral choices, we do not need to study ethics; all we need is a knowledge of God's commandments and a will to obey them.

R E F L E C T : *Do you agree or disagree with the idea that "for most of our daily moral choices . . . all we need is a knowledge of God's commandments and a will to obey them"? How do we develop this "will to obey"?*

The Subtlety of Lies

We have renounced secret and shameful ways; we do not use deception,
nor do we distort the word of God. On the contrary, by setting forth the truth plainly
we commend ourselves to every man's conscience in the sight of God.

2 CORINTHIANS 4:2

The lies we tell ourselves are the most subtle of all lies. Nobody wakes up in the morning and says to himself, "I think I shall lie to myself today." The deception happens in such a tiny fraction of a second that the self-deceiver is not even aware that he has lied to himself. What lies does he tell himself? One of them is the lie that *he* is not really lying when he tells a lie. Another is the lie that the moral law does not apply to him, at least not in this case. In short, people tell bold-faced lies about very important things and feel no guilt about their lying because they lie to themselves about what they are doing. Their problem is not with their heads but with their hearts.

PRAY: *Ask God to make you aware of any self-deception and to help you live a life of authenticity and obedience.*

MONDAY

The Spirit's Eye-Openings

We are witnesses of these things, and so is the Holy Spirit,
whom God has given to those who obey him.

ACTS 5:32

The Spirit of God is our eye-opener to the human situation that requires a decision from us. The moral law by itself is not enough to guide us. What we need is the ability to see what is really going on in the human circumstances to which we are trying to apply the moral law.

We must remember, however, that the Spirit is not like an eye surgeon; he does not remove our cataracts. Nor is the Spirit like an optometrist; he does not prescribe new lenses for our eyeglasses. The Spirit works on what lies behind our eyes. It is said that what we see lies 80 percent behind our eyes. It is that 80 percent that the Spirit works on.

PRAY: *Ask the Spirit of God to guide you through the decisions you make today, to be your "eye-opener" to the circumstances to which you are trying to apply the principles of Scripture.*

Taking Away Blinders

A rich man may be wise in his own eyes,
but a poor man who has discernment sees through him.

PROVERBS 28:11

Ordinarily, we see what we want to see. We do not want to see reality because we are afraid of what it might tell us. The Spirit, however, gives us courage and honesty to want to see the truth no matter how much we fear it. This is how the Spirit opens our eyes to reality: he takes the blinders of fear away.

Seeing reality for what it is is what we call discernment. The work of discernment is very hard. Reality is always deucedly complicated; any human situation has far more to it than first meets anybody's eye. No one has twenty-twenty discernment. This is why we need other people to tell us what they see in the same chunk of reality that we are looking at. This is why people of the church need to share their visions of reality *with* each other before they shout their judgments *at* each other.

APPLY: *Who can you count on to help you look at the "same chunk of reality" you're looking at and give you wise, godly counsel? If you don't have such a person in your life, seek to cultivate that type of relationship. Share this desire with the Lord, and trust that he will hear and respond to the desire of your heart.*

Listening to People

> *Those who look intently into the perfect law that gives freedom and continue in it—*
> *not forgetting what they have heard but doing it—*
> *they will be blessed in what they do.*

JAMES 1:25 TNIV

I discovered a long time ago that listening to people who see reality differently than we do is one of the most important parts of discovering the will of God for that reality. Nobody sees reality whole; we all need others to show us the parts of it that they see better than we do. Nobody sees reality with total accuracy; we all need others to correct our own vision. This is why we need to pray for patience to see what is really going on *before* we decide what God wants us to do about it.

PRAY: *Ask God for the patience and the diligence to seek out and engage with people who hold a different perspective on the world, and invite God to speak into that relationship.*

When Eyes Are Opened

If anyone has ears to hear, let him hear.

MARK 4:23

Consider what it was that opened Christian people's eyes to the fact that slavery was an evil thing. They had grown up listening to preachers who quoted passage after passage from the Bible to prove that slavery was not only the will of God but was a blessing to both the slaves and the masters. What persuaded them that the preachers were wrong? What persuaded them that slavery was a curse to both masters and slaves?

It was not a scholar's new interpretation of Bible texts. The conversion came only when their eyes were finally opened to see slaves for what they were— members of the same human family as the masters who owned them, fellow human beings who, like them, wept when they grieved and laughed when they were happy, who aspired to better things for their children and were as likely as any Calvinist to love the Lord their God. It took courage for people to see what they were afraid to see and hear what they did not want to hear.

PRAY: *Ask God to give you the ears—and the courage—to hear what you need to hear in order to more fully comprehend and follow the way of Christ.*

Right Time, Right Way

Speak the truth to each other,
and render true and sound judgment in your courts.

ZECHARIAH 8:16

How do we know the right time and the right way to tell the truth? How do we know when and how to tell a person that she is dying, or that her son has gotten himself in jail, or that her husband has lost his job, or that she has made a fool of herself, or that her little child has an incurable disease, or that his wife is having an affair? What we need more than anything else is the Spirit of love to open our eyes and ears to see and hear what is really going on in the heart and mind of the person to whom we are talking.

PRAY: *Ask God to open the eyes and ears of your heart as you offer counsel, encouragement or guidance today. Ask for discernment to know what to say, how to say it and how to practice the presence of God with people today.*

A Brand~New Ethic

If you really keep the royal law found in Scripture,
"Love your neighbor as yourself," you are doing right.

JAMES 2:8

God the Father has shown us what is right and what is good in his design for the good life in his world.

God the Son has shown us not a brand-new ethic but a more excellent way of following the old one—the way of an unselfish love that nudges us to do *more* than the law demands and to do it always with a will *to be helpful* to other people.

The Spirit of God opens our eyes to see and our hearts to hear the conflicting and confusing voices of the human situation that requires a moral decision.

These three assumptions about God formed the backbone of my life as an ethicist. They seemed right when I began, and they seem right to me still.

JOURNAL: *Write down your thoughts about each of the ethical assumptions about God contained in today's meditation.*

MONDAY

United with Christ

> *The Spirit himself testifies with our spirit that we are God's children.*

The apostle Paul says that we are affected by the event of two millennia ago, but not by being united with the Christ who was there then. Indeed, Christ is no longer a historical figure from whom we are separated by the years. He has become a life-giving Spirit who connects us with Christ as if he were our contemporary. The Holy Spirit, or the Spirit of Christ, is the link between us. Therefore, when his Spirit gets into our spirits, it is really Christ who gets into our spirits. The great gap of time between Jesus and us is bridged by the Spirit.

REFLECT: *In what ways do you see evidence of the Holy Spirit's presence in your life? How have you sensed the Spirit bridging the "great gap of time between Jesus" and your life?*

No Other Pleasure

Thanks be to God for his indescribable gift!

2 CORINTHIANS 9:15

I have two main feelings toward God these days: gratitude and hope. Both feelings keep slipping in and out of my spirit, one on the heels of the other. When gratitude comes, hope is right behind. If I am feeling grateful to God for the gifts he has given me, I at once start hoping that he will give the poor of our world more gifts to be grateful for. I feel ashamed to feel so good with what I have while most people on our planet feel so bad about the little they have. And my shame makes me very impatient with God. Which is all right, because impatience is one of hope's life signs.

I learned long ago that if anything can be better than getting a gift, it is the gratitude we feel for getting it. There is no other pleasure to compare with it— not sex, not winning a lottery, not hearing lovely music, not seeing stunning mountain peaks, nothing.

P R A Y : *Take time to pray in gratitude for gifts that you've been given—by our Lord, by members of your family, colleagues at work or others.*

Gifts with a Person Attached

A gift opens the way for the giver and ushers him into the presence of the great.

PROVERBS 18:16

I do not understand how people can be thankful for a gift if they have no person to thank for giving it to them. We teach our children to say thank-you to their grandmother for her birthday gift; why should we not teach them to say thank-you to God for the gift of their birth? (This thought is a gift from G. K. Chesterton.) Why should we not teach them that every new dawn of every new morning, every drop of rain, every budding tulip, every blade of grass, every lovely thought we think, every wonderful feeling we feel, every memory of pleasure past, every tingle of pleasure present, every touch of a loved one's finger, every hug from a laughing child, every note of a Mozart concerto, every coming home to our own place and people, every new hope that sees beyond a hard present—all of them are gifts with a Person attached.

JOURNAL: *Create a list of the diverse gifts of God for yourself, and express your thanks to the giver of those gifts.*

When God Comes Back

He has appeared once for all at the end of the ages
to do away with sin by the sacrifice of himself.

HEBREWS 9:26

C. S. Lewis said somewhere that when God comes back to earth it will be like having the author of a play called on stage after the final performance; the play is over, he takes his bow, the players leave, and the theater is swallowed in darkness. I do not much like his metaphor. I believe that the Author of the play will appear on stage not after the final performance, but before the first curtain rises. The players have been turning rehearsals into nasty fights about who gets the best lines and the prime spot on the billboard; the play has become a disaster, doomed before it gets off the ground. It is then that the Author shows up, his original script in hand and with the power to change self-seeking egos into self-giving artists. The theater is bathed in gentle light, the curtain rises, and the play begins a triumphant and endless run. Not the ending, but the new beginning—this is what I hope for.

REFLECT: *As you ponder the new heaven and the new earth to come, how do you picture it?*

A Universal Experience

He did not waver through unbelief regarding the promise of God,
but was strengthened in his faith and gave glory to God,
being fully persuaded that God had power to do what he had promised.

ROMANS 4:20-21

Hope is a universal human experience, and whether we hope as believers or as unbelievers, it always comes as a blend of three psychological ingredients. The first ingredient is a *dream*: we can hope only if we have eyes to see—albeit through a glass darkly—what it would be like for us if we got what we hoped for. The second is *desire*: we can hope only for what we want—want, indeed, with a passion. The third ingredient is *faith*: we can keep on hoping only so long as we keep on believing that our dream will come true and our heart's desire for it will be satisfied.

When it comes to hope that God will come and fix his world, I claim to have all three ingredients: a dream, a desire and a faith.

REFLECT: *Reflect on your own dreams, desires and expectance of a world made right by our Creator God.*

The Only Game in Town

Because of the LORD's great love we are not consumed, for his compassions never fail.
They are new every morning; great is your faithfulness.
I say to myself, "The LORD is my portion; therefore I will wait for him."

LAMENTATIONS 3:22-24

One thing is for sure, if God does not come to fix his world, nobody else can do it for him. To be blunt about it, his is the only game in town.

I put all my eggs in God's basket for one reason: Jesus died and came back to life again. Then he became the life-giving Spirit to give us, be it in driblets, a sampling of the good world we are waiting for. This is where the trolley stops. If it could be proven beyond doubt that Jesus did not come alive after he was murdered, we have lost our one and only reason for hoping that there can be a good future for the world. Without Jesus we are stuck with two options: utopian illusion or deadly despair. I scorn illusion. I dread despair. So I put all of my money on Jesus.

PRAY: *Thank God for his faithfulness, for raising Jesus back to life and giving his Spirit to intercede on our behalf. Express your gratitude for receiving, even in "driblets," a sampling of the good world we are waiting for.*

M O N D A Y

A Pretty Good Person

Those who feared the LORD talked with each other,
and the LORD listened and heard. A scroll of remembrance was written in his presence
concerning those who feared the LORD and honored his name.

MALACHI 3:16

Deep in every healthy person's heart simmers a longing to be a good person. A *pretty* good person, at least. Every now and then we sense a fine urge inside of us that leaves us unsatisfied with what we are. And, for a moment fled too soon, we feel the flutter of a longing always to be the person we were in that fleeting encounter with our truest self.

If you think you might be an exception, I want to ask you a simple question: How do you want people to remember you after you die? I mean people who matter to you. Maybe your children. People who know the sort of person you really are. Think about it. How do you want them to remember you? How we want to be remembered is a sure sign of the sort of person we really want to be.

REFLECT: *How do you respond to the question, "How do you want people to remember you after you die"? What does this tell you about the sort of person you really want to be?*

Your heart became proud on account of your beauty, and you corrupted your wisdom because of your splendor. So I threw you to the earth; I made a spectacle of you before kings.

EZEKIEL 28:17

Feeling good, looking good and making good are very good goods, but they make very bad gods. As gods they eventually leave us feeling like spent dreams on the soiled sheets of disenchantment. But plant them in the good of being good, and we may have what it takes to make a fine life for ourselves.

So it is time we look to our better dreams, our nobler inclinations, the set of our soul's main sails, or, in Alexis de Tocqueville's fetching phrase, the "habits of our hearts." Time to wonder what it would be like to be a pretty good person in a pretty spoiled world.

Pretty good people still sweat it out against some wild and some mild corruptions that inhabit their frail spirits. The best people I know are muddling their way through a mess of moral rubbish on the steep road to character. Good and bad crisscross through their circuits continually, thumbing their noses at each other as they pass. Sometimes the good signal is louder. Sometimes the bad. But the odds are better than even that they will hear the good signals most of the time.

REFLECT: *Reflect on the "habits of your heart." Which of them point to the nobler inclinations you possess? Which of them to the "wild" and "mild" corruptions? Ask God to set aside the moral rubbish on the steep road to character.*

Gratitude and Gladness

Although they knew God, they neither glorified him as God nor gave thanks to him,
but their thinking became futile and their foolish hearts were darkened.

ROMANS 1:21

Gratitude is our gladness. We were born to it.

Inside the itchy hankering of every heart stirs an aching need to feel grateful. We are heavy until we feel the lightness of gratitude. We hear the sweet music of joy only when we feel some awe and wonder and delight, and surprise, too, at being our own best gift. But once we have felt it, we know that there is no pleasure on earth like it.

My mother had a heavier way with gratitude. Whenever I groused about my lot in life, she whacked my conscience with this solemn bromide: "Lewis, you *ought* to be grateful." She was right, I suppose, to press gratitude into the mode of duty: we ought to be grateful.

Mother only echoed the wisdom of the ages. The roman sage Cicero called it the "mother of all virtue." And listen to the ancient stoic Seneca: "There was never any man so wicked as not to approve of gratitude and detest ingratitude."

REFLECT: *Is gratitude usually a duty or a delight for you? In what ways is gladness in life rooted in the discipline of gratitude?*

Obligations and Opportunities

Whatever you do, whether in word or deed, do it all in the name of the Lord Jesus,
giving thanks to God the Father through him.

COLOSSIANS 3 : 17

How can we put together the sure intuition that we have a duty to be grateful and the experience that duty seldom moves us an inch toward the joy of it? The secret lies in the difference between an ought of obligation and an ought of opportunity. "You ought to tell the truth on your income tax report"—there's an ought of obligation for you. "You ought to take advantage of this tax deduction"—here's an ought of opportunity.

We ought to be grateful the way we ought to applaud a great musician who has just set our hearts afire, the way we ought to laugh at a very funny joke, and the way we ought to hug someone we love. Life calls us to gratitude the way the sun says to the buried seed: "You ought to break out of your shell and come alive as the lovely flower you were always meant to be."

Giving and gratitude go together like humor and laughter, like having one's back rubbed and the sigh that follows, like a blowing wind and the murmur of wind chimes. Gratitude keeps alive the rhythm of grace given and grace grateful, a lively lilt that lightens a heavy world.

PRAY: *Ask God to create in your heart a rhythm of grace and gratitude that lightens what oftens feels like a heavy world—for others and for yourself.*

Giving Thanks

> Worship the LORD with gladness; come before him with joyful songs.
>
> PSALM 100:2

To give thanks is to give one's self to the giver who came tucked into her gift. Gratitude is our way of welcoming the giver, and thanks is our way of stitching an inch of ourselves alongside her.

A gift without a giver attached is a false thing. It is not really a gift at all, just something for nothing; and it does not move us to gratitude. An impersonal gift may be no more than a lure. We know what salespeople are up to when they remember us at Christmas with a bottle of perfume. We know what lobbyists are up to when they offer a Congress member a free vacation in Hawaii. Some people give gifts to people the way a fisherman offers a fly to a trout. We know what's going on; we've just gotten so used to the charade that we don't get upset by it.

But we never feel the gladness of gratitude when we get it.

REFLECT: *Have you ever received a gift for which you sensed there were strings attached? How did you respond? What does that tell you about the importance of your gift-giving to others?*

Possessed by Gratitude

Now my eyes will be open and my ears attentive to the prayers offered in this place.

2 CHRONICLES 7:15

Sometimes we are surprised by what we have known all along; the familiar suddenly glows with newness. I have walked down a street five hundred times without noticing a fantastic liquidambar—the only tree that turns a New England color in the Southern California autumn—and then, without expecting it, I see it one day for the beautiful gift that it is.

I live for a week feeling stressed and begrudging when suddenly, for no special reason, I am walloped with wonder that I should be alive, here and now, with thoughts in my head, feelings in my heart, visions in my mind. I am possessed by gratitude.

Not even a real gift gives a guarantee that we will be grateful for it. The giver does not have magic power. And the receiver cannot turn on gratitude the way she turns on a smile. We have limited control of the attitude of gratitude. All we can do is keep the windows open so that it can get in when it comes near.

REFLECT: *Think back on a time your eyes were suddenly opened to a gift that had been in front of you all along, unnoticed. What was your response? How can we nurture more attentiveness in our lives?*

MONDAY
Whispers of the Human Heart

He trusts in the LORD; let the LORD rescue him. Let him deliver him, since he delights in him.

PSALM 22:8

There have been times when, if someone told me that life is a gift, I would have wanted to give it back. There was so much about life that I hated, so much pain, that I could not locate grace enough to stir the ashes of gratitude. But I said thanks anyway, and saying it helped keep the window open.

You never know when saying something that you do not feel will prime the pump and get the feeling flowing. The line between pretending to feel something and beginning to feel it is, as C. S. Lewis put it, too thin for a moral bloodhound to sniff. Thanksgiving is the primal whisper of the human heart. And the whisper may be the prime that moves the waters.

REFLECT: *Have you ever given thanks to God for something even when you felt that everything was all wrong? How did whispers of gratitude in those times truly "prime the pump and get the feeling (of gratitude) flowing"?*

Help Along the Way

Strengthen the feeble hands, steady the knees that give way.

ISAIAH 35:3

The strongest and brightest of us are fragile as a floating bubble, unsteady as a newborn kitten on a waxed kitchen floor. If we keep our footing in the shaky space between our arrival and departure from this world, we owe our survival—not to mention our success—to many other people who held us up and helped us crawl or fly or just muck our way through. And to God, who keeps breathing life into our lungs the way a child keeps puffing air into a leaking balloon.

We take our every step in the energy of mercy. We breathe every breath in the atmosphere of grace. We think every thought, feel every feeling, through the power of creative love. We see each flower, taste each drop of water, sense the presence of each person around us, through the gift of consciousness. When we see all this with our inner eye, we will need no one to tell us we ought to be grateful.

JOURNAL: *Make a list of people to whom you owe your success, guidance and "survival." Thank God for knitting your life and theirs together.*

The Faces of Courage

Act with courage, and may the LORD be with those who do well.

2 CHRONICLES 19:11

You can show courage by advancing; you can show courage by retreating. You can show courage by dying for a good cause; you can show courage by living for a good cause. You can show courage by saying No to compromise; you can show courage by making a heroic compromise. You can show courage by throwing off your yoke; you can show courage by bearing it. Courage comes to life in almost any shape or form.

There are, however, two basic forms of courage. One is acting well at the risk of deadly danger. The other is acting well when troubles are already upon us.

Take the first form. We look danger full in the face and do what we have to do in spite of it. We make a move. By making it we risk loss to ourself. Maybe death. Maybe something else very important to our life.

Take the second form of courage. People show courage just by struggling long against present adversity. They do not risk death, they risk living. It takes a lot of courage just to hang on to life when the sullen days of a wearying winter are too long and dark to endure.

REFLECT: *What form of courage is most required of you today? Ask God to provide you with the courage you need to hang on to life or step forward into risk.*

Courage, Passive and Aggressive

Christ is faithful as a son over God's house.
And we are his house, if we hold on to our courage and the hope of which we boast.

HEBREWS 3:6-7

When sorrows whisper that living is a bigger burden than we can bear, it takes courage to look trouble full in the face and affirm our lives in spite of it. What we have here is *perseverance*, or what St. Paul was inclined to call *patience*. Plato called it *endurance*. Thomas Aquinas talked about a *passive* courage that is just as real as *aggressive* courage.

We often need this kind of courage as we get older, when our spicy juices turn to a sluggish syrup; when we feel in every joint a rusty resistance to healthy intentions; when our sexual drive is more memory than temptation; and we notice too often that too many of our old friends have died. It takes courage to celebrate life while numbering our days.

REFLECT: *Who in your immediate circle of friends or family stands out to you as a courageous person—and why?*

Making the Right Moves

Better to meet a bear robbed of her cubs than a fool in his folly.

PROVERBS 17:12

No matter what we do, to count as courageous we need the right motive for doing it.

Aristotle said, "It is for a right and noble motive that the courageous (person) faces dangers and performs the actions appropriate to courage."

We can run into a burning house to save a child, which is courageous. Or we can run into a burning house to save our record collection, which may be craziness. Those odd folk who drop themselves over Niagara Falls in a barrel are daredevils, sure enough, but few of us call them courageous. A woman may risk her life because she hates life and wants, consciously or unconsciously, to end it. And a man could run straight into a buzz saw because he doesn't know what he is doing. Risking everything does not count as courage unless there is a good reason behind it.

APPLY: *Using a concordance or other reference tools, search the Scriptures for all the uses of the words* courage *or* courageous. *What do you glean from the Bible's use of the words and the examples found in the lives of biblical characters?*

Fear and Hope

> *Be strong and take heart, all you who hope in the LORD.*
>
> PSALM 31:24

Hope gives us courage to do what we are afraid to do.

We fear and we hope at the same time. Fear lurks behind hope the way the dark side of the moon lurks behind its shining face. And hope answers fear the way the sun answers the darkness of the night.

An ordinary visit to a doctor is a little parable of fear and hope. We are afraid we might be sick, and we are afraid the doctor may tell us that we are very sick. But we have a hope that if we *are* sick, the doctor can cure us. Fear says, "Don't go, you may get bad news." Hope says, "Go ahead, he may find a way to heal you."

If it is hope that encourages, the loss of hope is the death of courage.

PRAY: *Ask the Lord to help you cling to hope even in the midst of the fears of life and to be a source of light in the face of darkness.*

M O N D A Y   *We Shall Overcome*

> I will praise you forever for what you have done;
> in your name I will hope, for your name is good.
> I will praise you in the presence of your saints.

PSALM 52:9

We get courage for living when we have hope that life will win.

Every historian I know agrees that people change their world only when they have hope that things can be better than they are. People do not revolt against tyranny because they are oppressed; oppressed people revolt when they have hope that freedom is theirs for the taking. Hungry people do not revolt because they do not have enough to eat; hungry people revolt when they have hope that their children can be fed.

Mother Teresa kept giving life to poor souls on Calcutta streets because she kept spotting human hope breaking through them. Ruby Bridges walked alone through walls of spite because she had hope that right would win the fight. Simple people marched for civil rights in step with a simple song of hope—"Deep in our hearts, we do believe, we shall overcome some day"—and singing it put courage in their hearts.

REFLECT: *As you look at the needs of your day, how can the witness of people like Mother Teresa and Ruby Bridges give you hope that change can take place?*

God Is on Our Side

What, then, shall we say in response to this? If God is for us, who can be against us?

ROMANS 8:31

The question of hope almost always ends with the question of God.

Sometimes I am almost sure that God has gone on leave of absence. And I fear that he is not on our side anymore. Hope answers that he is still here and that he is still on our side. God is on the side of life, not of death. God is on the side of love, not of hate. On the side of peace, against war. On the side of joy, against misery. This is hope's last stand.

This is what the resurrection of Jesus is about for me: hope for the ultimate victory of God. I am often afraid he may be losing the fight. But hope brings back a faith that he will win. My head lobs darts at my heart. But then I join the chorus when hopeful people sing:

Peace is going to win, brother.

Oh, yes, Lord.

Love is going to win, sister.

Oh yes, Lord.

Joy is going to win, children.

Oh yes, Lord.

Oh yes, Lord.

PRAY: *Express your thanks to God that he is still here, that he is not silent and that he is still on our side. Pray with thanksgiving for the resurrection of the Son of God, and the sending of the Holy Spirit.*

Courage in Community

I eagerly expect and hope that I will in no way be ashamed, but will have sufficient courage so that now as always Christ will be exalted in my body, whether by life or by death.

PHILIPPIANS 1:20

I have heard it said that of all sports the supreme test of character is the marathon run. Every runner is on his or her own, alone with terrible aches, alone with doubts, and alone, sometimes, with the secret longing to drop out, lie down and let the pain go away.

But when I watched my son Charlie run cross-country races, I learned that behind the lonely race was a runners' community. Off track the runners formed an inner circle of commitment to each other—a breed apart, not like other athletes. They knew it, and their sense of it made them comrades. At the end of the race the person who came in first would run back several hundred yards to plead with the stragglers to hang in and finish strong.

Nobody else can have courage *for* us. But behind individual acts of courage there is usually a community. Courage is contagious. It spreads when we get close to each other.

REFLECT: *What role does Christian community have in nurturing courage and hope within you? How can you be more intentional about seeking out community so that "contagious courage" can be more of a reality in your life?*

Staying True

In my integrity you uphold me and set me in your presence forever.

PSALM 41:12

Integrity is a bigger thing than telling the truth. It is about *being* a certain kind of person. It is about being people who know who we are and what we are, and it is about staying true to what we are even when it could cost us more than we should have to pay.

Think of yourself as someone who is writing a story out of the bits and pieces of your life. You are both the author and the main character.

To write a real story, the first thing we have to do is to own the one we are given to write. To own anything involves at least two things. First, we identify ourselves with what we own and say, "This is my story. If you want to know me, you must know my story; and if you know my story, you really know me. I *am* my story." Second, we take responsibility for what we own and say, "What comes of my story is up to me. This is my plot to take credit for, mine to take blame for, mine to own up to."

JOURNAL: *Write down elements of your own story out of "the bits and pieces of your life." Reflect on what it means to "own your story" and consider whether there are aspects of your story that you don't own, or have a hard time taking responsibility for.*

Owning Our Stories

Help us, O God our Savior, for the glory of your name;
deliver us and forgive our sins for your name's sake.

PSALM 79:9

We own our stories when we are willing to accept the parts we cannot control and then do whatever we can with the rest. We own our stories when we can admit to their ugly sides, their stupid and crazy sides. We own our stories, too, when we celebrate their beautiful aspects, their smart sides and their good sides. We own our stories when we keep holding on to them, even when we feel as if the story we are writing is a bore or gets so confusing we don't know what to make of it.

Nobody writes a simple story. We weave them with threads of our maniacally selfish streaks, our ugly impulses, our lust and our hate; but we also sew them together with the thread of love and courage and a simple ambition to make something of ourselves. We take ownership of one chapter and then another, each in its own time, each in its own way, until we round our story off, whole, in one piece.

JOURNAL: *What are the "beautiful aspects," the "smart sides" and the "good sides" of your own story? Be generous with yourself in your reflections.*

Working with Our Material

For if you forgive men when they sin against you, your heavenly Father will also forgive you.

MATTHEW 6:14

We can write honest stories only if we come to terms with the raw material we were given.

For some it all comes as a gift. For others childhood is a nightmare too horrible to remember. For almost all of us it is a mixed inheritance. But whether we remember them in thanks, or look back on them in rage, or recall them in a crosswind of conflicting emotions, our parents are the only parents God will ever give us, and the raw material we get from them is the only grist we will ever have for grinding out our stories.

If we have enough imagination, we may understand that our parents were limited by the raw materials they got from *their* parents. So we accept them as they were with an indulgent grace. And what we cannot understand or accept we may need to forgive. Indeed, for some, the toughest part of owning our stories is forgiving our parents for giving us such pain to begin our stories with. But if we are going to take ownership of our stories, we must forgive them in spite of everything—and then go on to write a good story out of whatever material they gave us to work with.

REFLECT: *What aspects of your story have you had a hard time understanding or accepting?*

MONDAY *The Residue We Carry*

> Her many sins have been forgiven—for she loved much.
> But he who has been forgiven little loves little.

LUKE 7:47

When we forgive, we free ourselves from bondage to bitter memories. We release ourselves from the acute, wrenching nausea of betrayal. We begin a process of healing. But we do not take away the wound. Not ever. Our pain has been grafted onto our very beings. We will carry a residue inside of us as long as we live. Any chance reminder can open the wound again. And the pain will come back for a while.

It takes courage to own our wounds, but we gain something important if we do. I believe that I have been more aware of other people's wounds since I discovered that the wound of my own pain is still part of me. I believe that anyone who is able to own the wounds that remain after forgiving someone who bruised them is better equipped to overcome similar pains in the future. And better able, too, to help other hurting people overcome theirs.

REFLECT: *What does it mean to "own our wounds"? What is the relationship between our ability to own our wounds and our ability to help other hurting people overcome theirs?*

Beginning a New Chapter

Your kingdom is an everlasting kingdom, and your dominion endures through all generations.
The LORD is faithful to all his promises and loving toward all he has made.

PSALM 145:13

Once we are well underway, we begin new chapters in our story by making significant commitments.

I speak a promise. "I will be there with you." Just a few words, mere words, words that I do not comprehend when I speak them; yet they flip from my lips straight into another person's memory to create a bond between us that neither of us will easily break. And so it is that my commitment nudges me into a new chapter of my story.

My commitments link what I am today with what I was in my past. When I remember them, I am remembering who I am.

Hannah Arendt reminds us in the closing chapters of her book *The Human Condition* that the stakes are high. "Without being bound to the fulfillment of our promises, we would be condemned to wander helplessly and without direction in the darkness of each person's lonely heart, caught in its contradictions and equivocalities."

REFLECT: *What are the promises or commitments you have made to others? What are the stakes involved in not fulfilling your commitments?*

Losing Our Integrity

> LORD, who may dwell in your sanctuary?
> Who may live on your holy hill? He . . . who keeps his oath, even when it hurts.

PSALM 15:1-4

To wander helplessly in the darkness of our own lonely heart, *caught* in its contradictions, trapped in equivocality. This is to lose our integrity.

The American psychologist Erik Erikson taught us that to write a real story a person needs to have "the capacity to commit himself to concrete affiliations, to abide by such commitments, even though they call for significant sacrifice." One way to weave our chapters into a whole story that we can make some sense of is to make commitments and to own the commitments we make. If we don't have the courage to own our commitments, we gradually lose touch with who we are and what our story is about.

PRAY: *Ask God for strength, courage and determination to own the commitments you have made.*

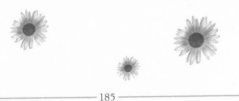

A Truth to Be Told

A friend loves at all times, and a brother is born for adversity.

PROVERBS 17:17

Not every truth I have in my head is mine to tell. A truth confided to me in trust, a truth I promised someone that I would not tell, is not my truth to tell. If my truth will needlessly diminish another or hurt another or tarnish another, it is not my truth to tell.

What *is* mine to tell? The truth that helps someone who needs it, this is the truth that is mine to tell. The truth another person needs in order to make a free decision, this is the right truth to tell. So is the truth that keeps an intimate relationship honest, or makes a sad person laugh, or reveals a beauty or a mystery that someone may never see if it is not told. And, more than anything, the truth to tell is the truth that another person is loved and forgiven, accepted, beautiful and worthy.

REFLECT: *How do you discern when a truth should be told? Use today's selection as a starting point: we should emphasize, more than anything, the truth that in Christ we are loved, forgiven and accepted.*

Telling the Truth Well

> *Be kind and compassionate to one another, forgiving each other,*
> *just as in Christ God forgave you.*

EPHESIANS 4:32

Two surgeons told the same truth to two patients. One of the surgeons leaned against the doorway as if he wanted to make a quick getaway, told his patient that his tumor was malignant and left him alone with his horrible truth.

The other surgeon sat down with the patient and his wife and told them a good many things about himself; he talked about his family, how he happened to get into surgery, and what he believed in. One of the things he believed in was the power of hope. Then he asked the patient to tell him a little about his life and about what he believed in. After they had gotten a feel for each other's story, he told his patient that his tumor was malignant, but that he, as a surgeon with years of observing such conditions, was not giving up hope.

To tell the truth well, we need to tell the right truth to the right person at the right time, but also in the right way.

REFLECT: *What about the second surgeon's truth-telling stands out to you? Is it the pace? his vulnerability in sharing a bit of his own story? simply his presence for the hearers of the bad news?*

A Place Called Integrity

In everything set them an example by doing what is good.

TITUS 2:7

Integrity is not an optional part of ourselves. A good car can lack air conditioning and still be a splendid automobile. But if we lack integrity, we lose our hold on the other components that go into the making of a pretty good person. Losing integrity is more like having our lungs cave in; everything else goes with them.

No living person has yet arrived whole at the place called integrity. If anyone tells you that he is a person of integrity, get a second opinion. We do well just to keep moving in the right direction. We have to check on our own intentions regularly, and see whether we are still moving on the journey or whether, at some shadowed station, we left the train and went off to nowhere. For, without integrity, anywhere is nowhere.

REFLECT: *Who in your life provides accountability on your journey toward integrity?*

M O N D A Y

Forgiving Ancient Wrongs

Get rid of all bitterness, rage and anger,
brawling and slander, along with every form of malice.

EPHESIANS 4:31

The only way back to control over our painful memories is the way of forgiveness. When we forgive, we surrender our basic human right to get even with the person who hurt us. But this surrender is not a defeat. It is the ultimate win.

When we forgive an ancient wrong, we set a prisoner free and discover that the prisoner we set free is us. When we forgive, we dance again to the melody of healing. When we forgive, we reclaim control of our lives from the slavery of a hurting memory.

PRAY: *If you are aware of painful memories that need the way of forgiveness, ask God to help you take that step of surrender which is really "the ultimate win."*

The Discipline of Surrender

Am I now trying to win the approval of men, or of God? Or am I trying to please men?
If I were still trying to please men, I would not be a servant of Christ.

GALATIANS 1:10

In the discipline of surrender we admit to ourselves that we try to get control of our own lives by controlling other people's opinions of us. And then we move on to the practice of surrender. We repeat over and over again to ourselves, alone and aloud, that God's love and our own integrity give us freedom to live without other people's approval. The very repetition of these words becomes a means of grace that brings them alive.

I confess to you that I would rather do almost anything than "gratuitous exercises" of the spirit. They feel artificial to me. But I know that when I refuse to practice, I end up losing control just when I need most to be in control. When I do practice, I am ahead of the game.

REFLECT: *Reflect on times you've tried to control your own life by controlling another person's opinion of you. What were the results? Ask God to help you gain the freedom to live without the unhealthy need for others' approval.*

Moments of Grace

*Let your conversation be always full of grace, seasoned with salt,
so that you may know how to answer everyone.*

COLOSSIANS 4:6

All around us, at any hour, people show up who ask us to do something about them. When they ask it, they give us a moment of grace.

We can write beautiful life stories out of our moments of grace.

Some people think that we make a good life by remembering the ancient moral principles that come to us from the past; when we have to make critical decisions, we simply hew to our principles. Other people think that we make a good life by dreaming dreams for the future; we set our sails and make all our decisions en route by asking which move will take us to where we want to go. There is something to be said for both points of view.

But there is another way of making a good life. The American scholar H. Richard Niebuhr suggested that we look at life as a conversation: as we enter each new situation, we engage in a conversation with it. It asks us a question. We listen. We make our response. And then we go on to another situation. Gradually we create our lives by the responses we give to the people we meet in all the different situations where we meet them.

REFLECT: *How do you view the making of a "good life"? How would the approach suggested by Niebuhr change the attentiveness with which you approach other people?*

Let us discern for ourselves what is right; let us learn together what is good.

JOB 34:4

After a career of watching people succeed and fail, psychologist Erich Fromm concluded that many people fail simply because they do not see what is happening around them or in them. And they do not see it because they are half asleep. "The paradoxical situation with a vast number of people today," he wrote in *The Art of Loving*, "is that they are half asleep when awake, and half awake when asleep." They do not wake up and see when they stand at a fork in the road and have to decide; they miss the moment of grace because they are not paying attention.

A person has to be awake to see where an innocent flirtation at five o'clock in the afternoon is almost certain to end by midnight. We have to be awake to notice that a charming persuader is manipulating us for his own ends. We have to be awake at dinner to sense that our companion has a burden that she wants us to notice without her having to say it.

The discerning person has to be awake to what is going on, the way a fast-ball pitcher needs to watch what a runner on first base is up to while he is also concentrating on the batter.

PRAY: *Ask God to help you grow in your attentiveness—to him, to yourself and to those around you—so you can respond faithfully in moments of grace.*

A Mystery's Revelation

> *Give your servant a discerning heart to govern your people*
> *and to distinguish between right and wrong.*

1 KINGS 3 : 9

To listen is to wait in silence for the revelation of a mystery. There is a mystery waiting to be revealed in all the voices that speak to us, the quiet voices, the loud voices, the angry voices, the friendly voices, the seductive voices, the ugly voices, the hateful voices and the loving voices. There is always something being said inside of what is being said. Standing still amid the voices that flow from the realities that touch our lives, waiting to hear what is there to be heard, to be heard in and under and over all the shouting and all the whispering— this is listening.

APPLY: *In your conversations today, pay attention to how well you are listening and being listened to. Make an effort to hear what is being said inside of what is said.*

More Than Raw Materials

I am your servant; give me discernment that I may understand your statutes.

PSALM 119:125

Most of us were born with healthy, vital, inquisitive, alert minds. And some of us have the gift of intuition besides. But these are only the raw materials. If we have them, we still need to practice them the way a great pianist like Arthur Rubinstein, at the very top of his genius, still kept his fingers in form by ever-lastingly running through some scales any fretful child has to bang away at when she first begins to play.

Discerning people are made, not born; and all of us have a chance to develop the skill for it.

APPLY: *What are the steps in the process of becoming a person who exhibits discernment on a consistent basis? Ask a friend or spiritual companion to practice the skill of discernment with you, using a book such as Gordon Smith's* The Voice of Jesus: Discernment, Prayer and the Witness of the Spirit.

M O N D A Y

The Route to Knowing

This is my command: Love each other.

JOHN 15:17

Experts used to tell us that if we expect to see things right, we have to be detached from what we are looking at. Objectivity! Staying aloof and drawing inferences by strictly monitored scientific methods—this was the route to knowing.

In his book *Personal Knowledge,* Michael Polanyi taught us to take a deeper look at how we get to know things. There are some things that we get to know only by getting personally involved with them. Only by being part of them, caring about them, having a deep feeling of attachment with them. In short, according to Polanyi, we can know some things only by loving them.

REFLECT: *What is your process of knowing? Does it resemble the detached, scientific variety? What appeals to you about the notion that we know some things "only by loving them"?*

> *The entire law is summed up in a single command:*
> *"Love your neighbor as yourself."*
>
> GALATIANS 5:14

I have often walked into ordinary human situations so insecure about myself that all I could see in them was the opportunity they offered me to fall on my face. As I entered their circle, my mind was fixed on myself and how I would come across. Would these people like me? Would they even notice me? Would they think my ideas are worth hearing? Or would they think that I am slightly ridiculous? As long as I kept thinking about how I was coming across to them, I could not see what was going on with them. I missed the moment of grace they offered me.

JOURNAL: *Over the next several days make note in your journal of how you respond in ordinary human situations at work, in your church and elsewhere. When have you been fixed on what others think of you and how you come across? When have you been able to capture the moments of grace they offered you?*

> *Be devoted to one another in brotherly love.*
> *Honor one another above yourselves.*

ROMANS 12:10

There are two ways that love helps me, now and then, to see real people through the filter of my insecurities.

One of them is a growing power to love myself enough to be thankful for what I am, and to forgive myself for what I am not. I feel this power intermittently, I admit, but I feel it enough to get my eyes off my anxieties about myself and focus on what is going on with other people.

Love also helps me to get outside of myself long enough to discover that the people whose favor I need so much are as weak and needy as I am. They are trusting me to care about them while I am struggling to see them through the haze of my own anxieties. If I discern them in their needs, I am getting the imagination to catch a moment of grace when it comes.

PRAY: *Ask God to help you discern the needs of others and catch a moment of grace when it comes today.*

Prone to Short-Sightedness

Let us discern for ourselves what is right; let us learn together what is good.

JOB 34:4

A good way to test our discernment is to share what we see with people who are looking at the same situation with us. They are seeing it through their own lenses, of course. They are as prone to short-sightedness as we are. They could be wrong. But they could also see something that we have missed. We need what the older philosophers called *docility*, a willingness to listen to people who may be able to correct our vision.

The primary reason people of goodwill disagree on the vexing and troubling matters of our time is not that some people are smart and others are stupid; nor is it because moral people are on one side and immoral people are on the other. We disagree mostly because we see things differently. And we see things differently because we filter everything through a grid of our own fears, pains, bitter or sacred memories, angers and loves. Even people who love well can see things differently.

APPLY: *How often do you bounce questions and ideas off a friend whom you know likely has a very different perspective than you do? Make an effort today to cultivate the virtue of docility.*

A Partial Discernment

> Even a fool is thought wise if he keeps silent,
> and discerning if he holds his tongue.

PROVERBS 17:28

Because our discernment is *always*—not sometimes, but always—partial, we need communities of shared discernment. We urgently need communities where we stifle the shouts and listen to each other, listen with the anticipation that every person who speaks to us may have seen something that we have missed. In a real community we do not listen to each other the way disciples listen to a guru. Or talk to each other the way the prophet proclaims the word to his followers. We will listen to each other because we have the grace to know that others may see reality just a little more deeply and a little more truly than we do.

APPLY: *Do you have a "community of shared discernment"? If not, seek out that type of community, and ask God to help you grow in wisdom and grace.*

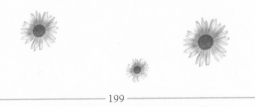

Imaginative Love

He who gets wisdom loves his own soul;
he who cherishes understanding prospers.

PROVERBS 19:8

People with cognitive discernment have a good sense of what is really going on. They see the little things that could make a big difference. They sense what people around them are feeling. They perceive how one thing is related to another, how one thing is different from another, and how one thing is more important than another.

But we need imaginative discernment to catch the moment of grace that offers us an opportunity to do something helpful and constructive. We still need the basic skills. We need to keep awake, keep an honest memory, keep our cool, keep listening, maintain some focus and respect our own intuition. But to become the sort of people who can be counted on in the moment of grace, we need to let what we see pass through the filter of imaginative love.

PRAY: *Ask the Lord to grant you discernment beyond what your human, finite mind can comprehend. Ask him to grant you a measure of imaginative discernment to "catch the moment of grace" offered to you this day.*

MONDAY

Knowing What Is Fair

Speak up and judge fairly; defend the rights of the poor and needy.

PROVERBS 31:9

Fair people try to be evenhanded, above board, square dealers, measure for measure all the way. When they divvy up whatever they have to share, they try to find a nice balance between what some people deserve and what other people need. Maybe they give more to those who need more. But when they give more to some, they do it not to show favor but to get things a little closer to equal for everyone.

In theory it is not difficult to know what is fair. When it comes to specifics, however, it is easier to recognize fair people by what they do not do than by what they do. As Aristotle said, we know best what is fair at the moment when we have been treated unfairly.

REFLECT: *"In theory it is not difficult to know what is fair."* Do you agree or disagree? *Why is fairness such a high value to each of us?*

A Careless Heart

Then you will understand what is right and just and fair—every good path.

PROVERBS 2:9

Love is an accident waiting to happen to any romantic with a careless heart. It needs no more effort than it takes a piece of dust to be swept up into a vacuum cleaner. Romantics wallow in metaphors: the right person will sit beside us and turn on a fountain to flush its crystal jets through all our spiritual arteries. A river of joy will bathe the lowlands of our being with such lush streams of pleasure that we, with our whole heart and soul, will want of all things in the world only to be swallowed in its shimmering depths. The romantic waits for love to happen the way a poor loser waits for a winning lottery ticket.

The test of reality, however, proves that we do not get lasting love by chance; we earn it the old-fashioned way—by working at fairness. Romance can keep love alive for a shining season; unfair love will freeze it by late fall.

PRAY: *Thinking of your closest family ties and friendships, ask God to help you work at fairness over the long journey of life.*

> *May your unfailing love be my comfort,*
> *according to your promise to your servant.*
>
> PSALM 119:76

We need fairness whenever we share our selves with each other. Fairness is at stake in every conversation, in every sharing of duties, in every argument, in every syllable of the communications of love. We need fairness in our trust; it isn't fair to let a person down. We need fairness in our talk; it isn't fair to use words that violate a person's feelings or betray a person's confidence. We need fairness when we divide the chores; it isn't fair to load one person with all the work it takes to keep a place the way lovers want to have it.

Lovers who have no bent for fairness end up hurting each other badly. We are wounded by unfairness when someone who loves us insults us in the presence of strangers. We are assaulted by unfairness when people who love us leave us in the cold while they tend to strangers. We are violated by unfairness when someone leaves us alone with only a painful memory of his broken promises. Unfair love is mean and cruel, and in the end is no love at all.

JOURNAL: *What types of unfair behavior have you suffered? What was the impact on you? Contrast that with times when someone has treated you with an uncommon degree of fairness. How did that impact you?*

Respecting Boundaries

Knowledge puffs up, but love builds up.

1 CORINTHIANS 8:1

Love is fair when it builds up both the lover and the beloved, when it increases both and diminishes neither, when it brings them close and lets them be separate, when it nourishes both and leaves neither wanting.

Fair love respects the boundaries of the other person's selfhood. It postpones our most legitimate desires to meet our loved one's needs. It declines every impulse to take advantage of a weakness. Fair love does not use ancient and forgiven wrongs against us. And our love is fair when we decline any pleasure that comes at the price of another's pain.

If we wrote down all the ways of fair love, the world would not hold the books we filled.

Love me well, but love me fair, or I would rather that you love me not at all.

JOURNAL: *Write down some of the ways you've encountered "fair love" with friends, family members, a spouse or perhaps even someone you did not know well but who extended a special kindness to you.*

Love Without Commitment?

Though one may be overpowered, two can defend themselves.
A cord of three strands is not quickly broken.

ECCLESIASTES 4:12

Fair love is a love that dares to make and cares to keep its commitments.

If you are inclined to keep your bags packed so that you can move on to greener pastures whenever love's pleasures grow stale, think about this: what would life be like if the best you could ever get from anyone was, "I'll be there if it suits me, but don't count on me"?

The fact is that love without commitment leaves lovers dangling in the shifting winds of uncertainty, which is fair to nobody. Commitment creates one small island of certainty in a heaving ocean where nothing is secure. When we make a commitment to another person, we give that person a claim to a secure place on the island.

When I make a commitment, I reach out into a future that neither of us can predict, and I give someone a right to believe that one thing is predictable—my presence with her. I stretch myself into circumstances that neither of us can control, and I give her the right to assume that one thing is under control—my intention to be present with her.

PRAY: *Ask God to help you maintain small islands of certainty in the relationships that are central to your life.*

The Heart of Love

May the words of my mouth and the meditation of my heart
be pleasing in your sight, O LORD, my Rock and my Redeemer.

PSALM 19:14

Love needs fairness the way a body needs a backbone. Love is soft. It needs a spine to make it work well.

The heart of love needs help from the mind of fairness. Love goes out to almost anything—God, dogs and almost all sorts of people. The mind of fairness tells us to match our loves to the soft thing we love.

The heart beats to the rhythm of bonding; the mind of fairness signals when to let the other person go.

The heart closes the circle around the people we love most; the mind of fairness tells us to keep the circle open a notch for others.

The heart is generous; the mind of fairness tells us how to give the right gift to the right person in the right way.

The heart of love forgives people who hurt us; the mind of fairness tells the heart to forgive carefully lest it hurt people with its forgiving.

REFLECT: *Very slowly and with space between each reading, verbalize Psalm 19:14 four to five times. Turn the verse into a meditation for your day.*

MONDAY

The Mark of a Good Person

We do not belong to the night or to the darkness. So then, let us not be like others,
who are asleep, but let us be alert and self-controlled.

1 THESSALONIANS 5:5-6

The best reason for being honest, for being courageous, for being discerning, and for having self-control, is to create relationships in which people love each other fairly.

For that matter, all our personal powers are linked together in a living network. Every virtue depends on the other. Without gratitude there can be no integrity; ingratitude falsifies life at the start. But integrity needs courage when honesty runs the risk of trouble. And courage needs discernment so that we can see what is going on and know when bravery calls us to act and when it calls us to stay where we are. But discernment needs self-control because when we fly off the handle we cannot see what is going on; and when we cannot see what is going on we usually end up making a mess of things. And then, at the end, all our linked powers lead us to a place where we can love each other fairly.

A pretty good person has a portion of all the powers. But the greatest of them all is love that is fair.

REFLECT: *Honesty, courage, discernment and self-control: which of the four represents the area you most need to work on as you continue in your journey of faith?*

Making Progress

> *You, O LORD, keep my lamp burning; my God turns my darkness into light.*
>
> PSALM 18:28

Life is all about making some progress at being what we are meant to be—the way being a bud is about becoming a blossom, or being a well-born colt is about becoming a thoroughbred racer. We have an inner itch to be more of what we were meant to be, and we never know but that we are on the verge of a breakthrough.

Goodness and badness will mingle in the veins of the best of us until we die. At one moment we will be more on the good side. At another moment we will feel a push toward the bad. None of us is going to get beyond our need for the grace of God and the charity of our friends. But with some help from both, we can become the sort of people who lean toward goodness. In other words, pretty good people.

PRAY: *Recognizing that "none of us is going to get beyond our need for the grace of God and the charity of our friends," offer a prayer of gratitude for the unending, abundant grace of our loving Father.*

Back to the Commandments

> *Honor your father and your mother,*
> *so that you may live long in the land the LORD your God is giving you.*
> *You shall not murder.*
> *You shall not commit adultery.*
> *You shall not steal.*
> *You shall not give false testimony against your neighbor.*

EXODUS 20:12-16

When Moses said, "Thou shalt not steal," he did not foresee the possibility of manipulating the price of common stock. When he said, "Thou shalt not kill," he did not envision the possibility that amniocentesis could tell a mother, three months or so after conception, that the baby she is carrying will likely die a horrible death within two years of its birth. So we must carry our facts—as we know them so partially—and our intelligence—as we use it so fallibly—back to the commandments and ask *how*, in the light of all we know and think about the life situation before us, we can obey the commandment in a way that promotes what the commandment is all about: fairness and love to all the people whom our decision touches.

REFLECT: *What perplexing decisions are you facing these days? What solutions promote fairness and love, self-knowledge and submission to God?*

A New Earth

What does the LORD require of you?
To act justly and to love mercy and to walk humbly with your God.

MICAH 6:8

Everyone in heaven and on earth wants justice. No man or woman, prince or peasant, saint or sinner has ever wanted injustice for himself or herself. Most people even want justice for others. Someone who claims to care nothing for others is immediately marked off as a misfit in the human family.

But although everyone praises justice, no people has ever achieved it. Justice is still a hope. When the apostle spoke of "a new earth in which justice dwells" (see 2 Peter 3:13) he depicted this as a good hope for a happy ending for God's human family.

God's own passion for justice shows itself throughout redemptive history. When he allied himself with Israel as an advance guard of the covenant people, he made justice a prime condition in the covenant with them. At its birth, the fundamental character of the community was established: "Justice, and only justice you shall follow, that you may live and inherit the land which the Lord gives you" (see Deuteronomy 16:20). Ever afterward, the acid test of the community's obedience to their covenant with God was: is justice done among the people?

REFLECT: *How is justice pursued through your local church? in your own family? by you as an individual? How does the admonition found in Micah 6:8 still apply to believers today?*

Beyond Intuition

> *"Cursed is the man who withholds justice from the alien, the fatherless or the widow."*
> *Then all the people shall say, "Amen!"*

DEUTERONOMY 27:19

Anyone who reads the Bible's call for justice already has a notion of what justice is. Aristotle observed that we know what justice is when we feel the wounds of injustice, and since every person on earth has, at some painful moment, joined the primeval chorus, "It's not fair!" we may assume that everyone has at least a primitive sense for the sort of thing that justice is. But wise people have sought to press beyond this intuition to elaborate on theories of justice. Do we take our cue from these? Does the Bible's sense for justice reinforce our common sense? Or does it exceed or complete or correct it?

Surely the Bible gives us a powerful motive for doing what we knew all along was ours to do.

PRAY: *Thank God for his high sense of justice and for the reinforcement we find in Scripture. Ask for the ability to do "what we know all along" is ours to do in pursuing justice, showing mercy and walking humbly with our God.*

The Justice of God

God presented him as a sacrifice of atonement, through faith in his blood . . .
to demonstrate his justice at the present time,
so as to be just and the one who justifies those who have faith in Jesus.

ROMANS 3:25-26

God's justice gives more than ordinary justice gives. At the heart of the gospel, God's kind of justice appears to be a total reversal of ordinary justice. Certainly that is how it looked to the first-century Jews, with their powerful sense of divine justness. For according to the good news, God does *not* give people what they have coming to them but what they do not deserve. He gives aliens the status of children, and sinners the status of righteous persons.

To those who objected that the idea of a God who played fast and loose with justice was blasphemy, Paul replied that the God of grace did not slacken justice; indeed, God justified the ungodly precisely "to prove at the present time that he is just" (Romans 3:26). The gospel of grace was not a reckless rumor that God no longer cared about justice; it was final proof that he is just.

MEDITATE: *Reread several times and reflect on the sentence, "For according to the good news, God does not give people what they have coming to them but what they do not deserve." How is this gospel of grace final proof that God is just?*

MONDAY *Love Seeks, Love Gives*

> *"This is my commandment, that you love one another as I have loved you."*
>
> JOHN 15:12 NRSV

Love is a power that rises from our soul's need; it is also a strength that flows from our soul's fullness. It drives me to seek another for my sake; it moves me to help another for his or her sake. Love seeks and love gives. Can love be one thing when it moves on two such different tracks?

We live by two separate powers, and we call them both love. We may set them apart by adding adjectives, as C. S. Lewis did, and name them "need-love" and "gift-love." Or we may use the Greek words, as theologians do, and call our two loves *eros* and *agape*—eros being the power that drives us to satisfy our own deepest needs, and agape the power that moves us to satisfy the needs of another. Both of them are the strength of life. Without either of them, our humanity wrinkles and withers like dead fruit. But they are not the same.

APPLY: *"Love seeks and love gives. Can love be one thing when it moves on two such different tracks?" For a more thorough exploration of the subject, consider reading C. S. Lewis's* The Four Loves *(or listening to the audiobook edition).*

The Command of Love

This is love: not that we loved God,
but that he loved us and sent his Son as an atoning sacrifice for our sins.

1 JOHN 4:10

The love we meet in Jesus Christ is *agape*, gift-love, the current that bears us to others for their sakes. This love is not our seeking, not even our seeking of God, but God's giving his very Son to help us. God's love becomes our love when he invades the center of our being, when God who is love "abides in us and his love is perfected within us" (see 1 John 4:12). He becomes our power of love to move toward persons who need us.

Love as power may enable us to do what God expects of us, but it is the command of love that tells us what to do. Love is what all other duties are about. Love ultimately explains *why* we ought to do all the things we ought to do.

PRAY: *Offer God thanks for his gift of love through Jesus, and for the power of the Holy Spirit to move us in love toward others who need us.*

How Did Jesus Love Us?

*The Son of Man did not come to be served, but to serve,
and to give his life as a ransom for many.*

MATTHEW 20:28

Jesus' love for us is God's norm for our loving: "This is my commandment, that you love one another as I have loved you." Rather than listing rules for the loving life, he made his own life the authoritative model for our loving. So we need ask only one simple question: How did Jesus love us?

Love moved Jesus to help people. No doubt Jesus *felt* for people, but his love came to life most clearly when he acted. He came "to give his life as a ransom for many," to take away our sins and bring us good from God, to liberate us from the devil and make us free. And he did what he said he had come to do.

JOURNAL: *Ponder the question "How did Jesus love us?" Journal a list of responses to the question.*

Going Beyond Virtue

*The tax collectors and "sinners" were all gathering around to hear him.
But the Pharisees and the teachers of the law muttered,
"This man welcomes sinners and eats with them."*

LUKE 15:1-2

Love *moved Jesus to help all people.* Love made Jesus indiscriminate. He excluded none; indeed, he seemed to go out of his way to embrace the scandalous sinners who were repugnant to the righteous folk. He moved beyond family ties to claim a motley crowd as his brothers and sisters (Matthew 12:48). He dismissed ethnic identity to embrace the despised Samaritans (John 4:39). Going beyond virtue, he forgave sinners (Luke 19:7). As God's perfection made him willing to let the rain fall on the just and unjust alike (Matthew 5:43), the same disregard for differences marked Jesus' life of love. Love made him the man for *all* others.

PRAY: *Thank God for his indiscriminate love, as expressed through Jesus Christ.*

The Sweet Taste of Victory

Whoever wants to become great among you must be your servant,
and whoever wants to be first must be your slave.

MATTHEW 20:26-27

Love moved Jesus to help all people for their sakes. Jesus came "not to be served, but to serve and thus to give his life as a ransom for many." Is it possible, Dag Hammarskjöld once mused, that Jesus did it all "yet for his own sake—in megalomania?" What seems like sacrifice may have been an investment in future pleasure. Perhaps he was savoring the anticipation of the sweet taste of victory and of the applause for his global coup. But Jesus' manner does not encourage us to ascribe such self-seeking erotic motives to him. His love seemed to drive him to us for our sakes, so that we could be saved.

Of course, Jesus cherished the joys that followed final victory; the thought of them sustained him in his time of ultimate suffering. But knowing he would enjoy the results does not mean that he paid the price only to win a crown for himself. We must believe that he suffered *for our sakes*. He was the man *for* all others, for their sakes.

REFLECT: *How would the gospel story change if Jesus had come and died and risen back to life "only to win a crown for himself"? Offer thanks to our God that he suffered for our sakes—for your sake.*

God So Loved the World

God did not send his Son into the world to condemn the world,
but to save the world through him.

JOHN 3:17

Love moved Jesus to help all people for their sakes without regard for cost. To provide the help we needed most, God had to give us himself. "God so loved the world that he gave his one and only Son" (John 3:16). Love moved him toward us for our sakes; and our great distance from him meant love could set no limits. So, although Jesus "was in the form of God . . . (he) emptied himself, taking the form of a slave . . . and being found in human form, he humbled himself and became obedient to the point of death, even death on a cross" (Philippians 2:7-8 NRSV).

Two moments in history signal the price of love: the moment of Jesus' birth and the moment of his death. In the light of these events, we must think of gift-love as a push toward ultimate sacrifice. Moved by love to help us for our sakes, he was committed to do whatever had to be done to help us.

REFLECT: *"Two moments in history signal the price of love: the moment of Jesus' birth and the moment of his death." Reflect on how these two events portray the price of love. Thank God that Jesus came not to condemn but to save—regardless of the price he would have to pay.*

M O N D A Y

The Goodness of Life

> *The LORD is my strength and my shield; my heart trusts in him,*
> *and I am helped. My heart leaps for joy and I will give thanks to him in song.*

PSALM 28:7

A deep need for joy leads us to seek a feeling of being one with the goodness of life. The Westminster Confession gives a theological slant to this; our true destiny, it says, is to "glorify God and enjoy him forever." John Calvin said that no one can know God without knowing himself; it is equally true that we cannot enjoy God without enjoying ourselves; we cannot even want to enjoy him unless we want to enjoy ourselves. All those texts in the Bible that command us to rejoice in the Lord are telling us to feel the goodness of our life.

REFLECT: *What impact would it have on your life if you daily embraced the idea that our chief end is "to glorify God and enjoy him forever"?*

The Rule of Honor

> *Honor your father and your mother, as the LORD your God has commanded you,*
> *so that you may live long and that it may go well with you*
> *in the land the LORD your God is giving you.*

DEUTERONOMY 5:16

Honor is the unsentimental moral nucleus within the complex relationships between any child and his parents. From the day the child is born to the day the parents die—and even reaching beyond their grave as a relationship to an ineradicable memory—everything in the relationship changes except the moral duty of honor.

The rule of honor is probably as universal as any human duty. No child, young or old, ought ever to dishonor his parents. In every culture, parents believe in their right to be treated with respect by their offspring. Plato probably registered a universal ethic when he said that on the scale of human decencies honor to parents is second only to piety toward God. But absolute as we admit it to be and universal as we imagine it to be, honor to parents is a duty that shifts and slips in our hands as we try to examine what it calls us, young or old children, to do.

REFLECT: *In what ways have you honored—or did you honor—your parents well? In what ways was extending honor a challenge? Why would this "rule of honor" be such a universal one?*

Refusing to See

> *Since the creation of the world God's invisible qualities—*
> *his eternal power and divine nature—have been clearly seen,*
> *being understood from what has been made, so that men are without excuse.*

ROMANS 1:20

If believers are tempted to deceive themselves about evil, unbelievers are equally tempted to deceive themselves about God. In Paul's eyes, unbelief is at its core an exercise in self-deception. God is so close to every person that denying him is like denying the sun at high noon. He scratches at every person's soul. He displays himself unmistakably in creation. He is there, in full view; there is no escaping him. But many sinful humans refuse to "see" him even though they cannot help seeing him; they know and they refuse to know. At some moment that slips by them unfelt, they choose not to know what they cannot help knowing. "So they are without excuse; for although they knew God they did not honor him as God" (see Romans 1:20-21). Unbelief is not merely a point of view, nor mere ignorance, but self-deception, a refusal to face up to the truth that lies plain before the heart.

REFLECT: *What reasons have you encountered for not believing in God? If "God is so close to every person that denying him is like denying the sun at high noon," why do so many not believe?*

Woe to you . . . hypocrites! You are like whitewashed tombs,
which look beautiful on the outside
but on the inside are full of dead men's bones and everything unclean.

MATTHEW 23:27

Truthfulness is a straight line between what we say and what we *are* as much as between what we say and what we *think*. It touches our being as it touches our thinking. We all draw profiles of our selves with the messages we send to others—no matter whether the medium be words or actions. The moral question is whether we intend the profile to look like what we really are.

Truthfulness about what we are may be even more important than truthfulness about what we think. Being a hypocrite seems worse to most people than merely being a liar. Phoniness, pretense, dissimulation—these are awesome accusations against any human life. Jesus scourged the shams of his day: "You are like whitewashed tombs, outwardly appearing beautiful, but full of dead men's bones and all unclean within. So you also appear outwardly righteous to man, but within you are full of hypocrisy and iniquity" (see Matthew 23:27-28). Being "full of iniquity" may be the common lot of sinners; but acting out a charade of virtue makes iniquity doubly nauseous.

PRAY: *Ask the Lord to help you maintain an authentic witness, ensuring that the outward profile of your life is indeed who and what you really are.*

Many a Conflict, Many a Doubt

Into your hands I commit my spirit; redeem me, O LORD, the God of truth.

PSALM 31:5

Truthfulness of being is an ideal we struggle toward. It is hard for us to be whole—inside and out—because we are complicated and confused within. We do not express our real selves because we do not know who our selves are. In a sense we are like the demon-possessed man whom Jesus healed. When Jesus asked him to identify himself, he said: "My name is Legion, for we are many" (Mark 5:9).

Dmitri Karamazov, feeling like a man torn apart, said: "Man is too complicated, I'd have made him simpler." How fatuous was Polonius's admonition to Laertes: "To thine own self be true. . . !" What Hamlet cried for was someone to tell him who his own self was. We are all only on the way toward our real selves. On the way, as the hymn writer put it, we are assailed by "many a conflict, many a doubt."

REFLECT: *Why is the ideal of truthfulness such a struggle?*

A Patient and Delicate Art

Love does not delight in evil but rejoices with the truth.

1 CORINTHIANS 13:6

The final moment in our clumsy try for truthfulness comes when our message finds its way into a listener's mind. But what he hears is not what comes from our mouths. Before he hears, he filters the message through an internal grid created by his own past impressions and current feelings. In the closet of his own subconscious, ghosts long hidden interfere with our message before it gets to his mind. By the time he hears our message, its shape has been slightly changed. What he hears is never exactly what we say. Thus, our truthfulness can become his falsehood.

And so we must listen to how our neighbor responds to what we say. If we do not listen we cannot know what he has heard, and if we do not know what he has heard we really do not know whether we have been effectively truthful. We cannot speak and run if we want to be truthful.

Listening is a patient and delicate art. It is not as if we can listen only once and be done with it. A counterpoint to Paul's "love rejoices in the truth" is this: "love listens long."

PRAY: *Ask God to enable you to fine-tune the delicate, patient art of listening.*

M O N D A Y *A Reliable Road Map*

The precepts of the LORD are right, giving joy to the heart.
The commands of the LORD are radiant, giving light to the eyes.

PSALM 19:8

If my assumptions are right, we are not stuck with having to improvise new solutions to every moral problem we encounter. There is a pattern that we can have in our heads beforehand. Nor do we have to keep our ears cupped constantly for the latest word from heaven. God has already delivered his basic directions.

We have a road map at our disposal. It shows only the main roads, to be sure. The commandments do not tell us everything we need to know as we face concrete decisions. But they provide direction, and they give us a bias. They lay out some of the most important *sorts* of things we ought to do in some of the most important zones of human life. The specifics are not always included in the map. Whatever extra help we get—sound reason, intuition or hints from the Spirit—can be tested by using the main thoroughfares as reference points.

APPLY: *Think of the Scriptures as a map at your disposal with the main roads for decision-making marked. Study it and pray over the precepts you see there. Ask the Holy Spirit to guide you as you face moral decisions, trusting that the Word will be a light unto your path.*

Moral Commandments

*I, the LORD your God, am a jealous God, . . . showing love to a thousand generations
of those who love me and keep my commandments.*

EXODUS 20:5-6

Justice and love are the two absolute moral commandments. They cover every conceivable human situation. There is no nook or cranny in our lives together in which we may ignore the demands of justice and love. Everything we do must be fair; if it is not fair, it is not right. And everything we do must be helpful, or at least not hurtful; if we mean it to hurt and not help people, it is not right. Justice and love form a kind of moral counterpoint in life. Justice holds us back in respect; it tells us to let people be what they are and have what they have. Love pushes us toward people in care; it tells us to get into people's lives so that we can help them be what they ought to be and get what they ought to have. Justice tends to urge us to keep the rules, especially the "thou shalt not's." Love translates the negative commands into positive invitations to creative helpfulness. Justice and love are the absolutes of life to which the other commandments point; the other commands are valid because they direct us to embody justice and love in the complex realities of human life.

PRAY: *Ask our Lord to enable you to embody justice and love in all of your human interactions. Invite the Spirit of God to translate negative commands into "positive invitations to creative helpfulness" toward others.*

Two Mistakes We Make

A fool spurns his father's discipline, but whoever heeds correction shows prudence.

PROVERBS 15:5

We all have critics; I have had a fair share of them in my time. All of us have people around us who tell us whether we dress right, talk right, think right or do right. Critics can make us feel guilty, or ashamed, or just plain incompetent if we let them. So one of the most important lessons about life that I, for one, am still learning, and maybe you are too, is this: how to cope with our critics.

There are two mistakes people often make when they are trying to cope with their critics. One mistake is to ignore them. But the trouble with ignoring our critics is that we may discover that they were right and that we would have been better off if we had listened to them. So it is a mistake to ignore our critics. On the other hand, it is an even bigger mistake to take them too seriously, to let them have the last word, as if they were our judges and were always right. The trick, then, is to listen to our critics but never, never let our critics be our judges.

REFLECT: *What is the difference between a "critic" and a "judge"? Why should we listen to our critics—but not let them be our judge?*

Those who have been given a trust must prove faithful.
I care very little if I am judged by you or by any human court; indeed, I do not even judge myself.
My conscience is clear, but that does not make me innocent. It is the Lord who judges me.

1 CORINTHIANS 4:1-4

A critic is one thing. A judge is another. Critics give us their own opinion, and it is up to us to take it or leave it. But judges are different; when they deliver their judgment, we have no choice, we simply have to take it. This is why I say: listen to your critics, but never let them be your judges.

The apostle Paul had his share of critics, and what he said to his critics has always been helpful to me. I recommend it to you. You can find his words in the New Testament at the very beginning of the fourth chapter of 1 Corinthians. "With me it is a small thing that I should be judged by you or anybody else for that matter. I do not even judge myself. It is the Lord who judges me."

You will notice that he had three kinds of critics: first, other people; second, himself; and third, the Lord. Three critics. We have the very same ones: other people, our own selves and the Lord.

PRAY: *Thank God for the fact that for those of us in Christ Jesus there is now no condemnation, no judgment.*

Critics, Not Judges

Judge nothing before the appointed time; wait till the Lord comes.
He will bring to light what is hidden in darkness and will expose the motives of men's hearts.
At that time each will receive his praise from God.

1 CORINTHIANS 4:5

Let's talk about our human critics: Our friends. People who go to our church. Our mothers. Even our own children. They can criticize us for just about everything. The apostle's critics, for instance, were carping at him for the way he carried on his missionary work. How did he respond? He simply said: "I am listening. I hear what you are saying. What you say matters to me. But when the chips are down, and you have had your say, your words are never the last word for me. You are not my judges."

When we let our critics become our judges, we let them decide whether we are good enough or beautiful enough to be loved and accepted.

REFLECT: *How do you handle your "human critics"? Seek, like the apostle, to listen to your human critics, to hear them but not let them be your judge.*

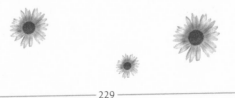

Critics Are a Blessing

All a man's ways seem right to him, but the LORD weighs the heart.

PROVERBS 21:2

Very often we have the hardest time when our critics are the very people we love and admire.

When I was in college, I had a wonderful teacher whom I greatly admired. And I wanted his approval above almost everything else. And if I did not have his approval, I would be crushed. In short I was letting my professor and critic be my judge. It took me a long time to say to myself: "I want him to be my critic; I will always take his opinion seriously. But I will not let him be my judge." I can tell you that the day I decided that my college idol would not be my judge, I found a new freedom to follow my own path without worrying about what he thought of what I was doing.

Critics are a blessing. We can all profit from them. But they can be a curse if we let them be our judges.

REFLECT: *Who are the people in your life from whom you can easily and gratefully receive constructive criticism?*

MONDAY

Taking Stock of Ourselves

Each one should test his own actions.
Then he can take pride in himself, without comparing himself to somebody else.

GALATIANS 6:4

God has made us with the ability to examine our own lives, to take stock of ourselves and be our own critics. The only way we will ever improve our lives is by being critical of ourselves. But, oh, we make a huge mistake if we become our own judges.

The apostle Paul knew this, so when he refused to let his critics be his judges, he added these words: I do not even judge myself.

It is important here to recall the difference between a critic and a judge: a critic gives you his or her opinion, and you can accept it or you can reject it. But when a judge pronounces his or her judgment, you are stuck with it.

REFLECT: *Take time to examine your patterns of self-criticism. Are they healthy? Or do they lean more toward self-judgment? Ask God to help you honestly examine your own life without slipping into unhealthy self-judgment.*

Our Blurred Vision

The heart is deceitful above all things and beyond cure.
Who can understand it?

JEREMIAH 17:9

The apostle was his own toughest critic. He took the measure of his own life and criticized himself very honestly. He said, "I find that I often do the very things that in my deepest spirit I do not really want to do. And I often fail to do the very things that, deep in my spirit, I really want to do" (see Romans 7).

Yes, the apostle was his own toughest critic. And he urged us to examine ourselves and be critical of what we see in ourselves. But be our own judges? Not on your life.

We are simply not competent to judge ourselves. When we take stock of ourselves, we tend to see what we want to see. When we are feeling good about ourselves, we want to see only the good things about ourselves. When we get down on ourselves, we actually look for bad things in ourselves. How we see ourselves is always blurred by the mood we are in. When we feel good about ourselves, we are too easy on ourselves. When we feel down, depressed, we are too hard on ourselves. The Bible says that all our hearts are deceitful, and they never deceive us so badly as when we are trying to examine our own selves.

PRAY: *Ask God to help you faithfully and regularly examine your life, free of both deceit and self-judgment.*

A Careful Judgment

This righteousness from God comes through faith in Jesus Christ to all who believe.
There is no difference, for all have sinned and fall short of the glory of God,
and are justified freely by his grace through the redemption that came by Christ Jesus.

ROMANS 3:22-24

I worry about people who, when they look inside themselves, always come up feeling smug, and thoroughly pleased with themselves. I also worry about people who look inside themselves and come up feeling as if their souls were cesspools. Neither of them has seen themselves for what they really are.

Their mistake is not that they criticize themselves. Their mistake is that they judge themselves. I know good people who are going through life judging themselves to be flawed and blemished and hopeless persons. Yes, I worry about good people who judge themselves and always find themselves wanting. On the other hand, I have known people who made a living by lying and cheating and stealing who convinced themselves that they were really models of good character. Yes, I worry about people who judge themselves and always find themselves innocent.

REFLECT: *Reread the Scripture passage above. Contemplate how this justification through the grace of Jesus Christ can give us confidence as we stand before the God who "is qualified to be our judge."*

God Is Our Judge

But it is God who judges: He brings one down, he exalts another.

PSALM 75:7

The apostle not only refused to let his human critics be his judges, he would not let himself be his own judge. But now comes the clincher. It was not as if he refused to be judged by anyone. He had a judge and told his critics who his judge was. He said: "My judge is the Lord" (see 1 Corinthians 4:4).

Think for a moment. God is qualified to be our judge because he knows us right down to the core, knows everything there is to know about us, good, bad and indifferent.

How can we live with the one critic who really has the competence to be our judge? For myself, I have found that the way to live with my divine critic is to know that whenever he judges me, he also loves me, forgives me and accepts me. Nothing I have ever done or ever will do can persuade God to reject me.

Jesus himself had critics who judged him to be deserving of the death penalty. But what his judges did not know was that when they condemned Jesus to death, God himself was in Jesus bearing their judgment. And since that moment when God was judged, he is the God who forgives.

APPLY: *For further reflection on the issue of criticism, consider reading the brief booklet by John W. Alexander and Stephen A. Hayner titled* Criticism: Giving It and Taking It.

The Love at Mount Calvary

"Has no one condemned you? . . . Then neither do I condemn you," Jesus declared.
"Go now and leave your life of sin."

JOHN 8:10-11

If anything is clear after a searching look at what God expects of ordinary people, it is that the moral standard for human beings remains an ideal. After learning what God expects of us, we must face up to our private and public history of failure. Only a complacent soul enjoys a feeling of success when he thinks deeply about mere morality. What needs to be said to this human situation is simply that the God who commands is also the God who forgives.

The gospel of grace releases us from the guilt of failure and opens new possibilities for a new effort. Moreover, it offers a new relationship with the Commander. He who pointed us to his design for living at Mount Sinai embraces us with his love at Mount Calvary. He who pins us down with demands at every nook and cranny of life frees us from any and all condemnation.

What God expects of ordinary people is obedience born of gratitude; what God gives ordinary people is forgiveness born of grace. Once forgiven, we hear his commands not as a burden but as an invitation to enjoy our humanity, and in our joy to glorify our Creator.

PRAY: *Pray, thanking God for the forgiveness born of grace; for release from the guilt of failure.*

Making a Hard Decision

Bear with each other and forgive whatever grievances you may have against one another.
Forgive as the Lord forgave you.

COLOSSIANS 3:13

Somebody you counted on let you down. Somebody you trusted betrayed you in your trust. Somebody who promised to take care of you, instead took advantage of you. The hurt goes deep. What makes the pain worse is that you were wronged. You did not have it coming. Nobody deserves to be treated the way you were treated. It was not fair.

There is no delete button for the past. You are stuck with it. You cannot forget what happened. You cannot erase it from your mind. It is like a video tape sewed inside your head. And every time it plays its rerun, you feel the pain all over again.

Now you have to make the hard decision. Do you want to spend the rest of your life with a pain that you did not deserve to get in the first place? Or do you want to be rid of it, healed, freed from it, so that you can go on with your life without that painful memory shadowing you? There is one way to heal yourself. It is not one way among many. It is the *only* way. God invented it. It did wonders for him and does wonders for us. We call it forgiving. And God tells us to try it for ourselves. "Forgive each other," the Good Book says, "as God in Christ forgave you."

REFLECT: *Why would forgiveness be considered the "one way to heal yourself" of hurt and the shadows of painful memories?*

MONDAY

Is Forgiving Fair?

Forgive us our sins, for we also forgive everyone who sins against us.
And lead us not into temptation.

LUKE 11:4

People have said to me, "Forgiving is just not fair. Why should I have to forgive the lout who did me wrong and let him off Scot-free as if it never happened? That just isn't fair," they say.

When they say that forgiving is not fair, I tell them that forgiving is the only way to be fair to yourself. Would it be fair to you that the person who hurt you once goes on hurting you the rest of your life? When you refuse to forgive, you are giving the person who walloped you once the privilege of hurting you all over again in your memory.

Remember this: The first person to get the benefits of forgiving is the person who does the forgiving. It's so important that I want to say that again: The first person who *benefits* from the forgiving is the person who *does* the forgiving. Forgiving is, first of all, a way of helping yourself to get free of the unfair pain somebody caused you. The most unfair thing about unfair pain is that you should go on suffering it in your bitterness and misery when there is such a simple remedy for it.

So if you think forgiving is unfair, let me tell you that once you've been wrongly hurt, forgiving is the only way to be fair to yourself.

REFLECT: *Why is forgiving one who has done you wrong "the only way to be fair to yourself?"*

A Way Out of Pain

So watch yourselves. If your brother sins, rebuke him, and if he repents, forgive him.

LUKE 17:3

Let me tell you what one woman learned about not being a doormat and still being a forgiver. I was a guest on a radio talk show one time, and a lady called in to tell us about how she had suffered the worst thing that could happen to a mother. A drunk driver in her neighborhood swerved his car out of control and hit and killed her three-year-old little girl who was playing on the grass near the curb.

As soon as she hung up, another woman called to say she had to speak to the first caller because the very same thing had happened to her. She said that for two years she lived in the fog of terrible rage.

Well, after living in the misery of her blind, unhealed rage for two years, she woke up to the fact that the drunk who killed her son was now killing her inside a day at a time, killing her soul. She was wise enough to go and see her priest who listened to her story and told her what she already knew, that the only way out of her pain was to set out on the journey of forgiveness. But he said there was something they had to do first. They had to begin a chapter of Mothers Against Drunk Driving in their town. They had to make it known that if you forgive a drunk driver it does not mean that you must tolerate drunk driving.

REFLECT: *The journey of forgiveness often includes doing something constructive with one's grief and pain. Why is this often an important part of one's way out of pain?*

Forgivers, Not Fools

*If we confess our sins, he is faithful and just and will forgive us our sins
and purify us from all unrighteousness.*

1 JOHN 1:9

Some people think that if you forgive somebody you once trusted, it means that you have to go back into the same relationship with him or her that you had before. If she was a friend who made a practice of betraying you, forgive her and be friends again. Not a good idea. Forgivers do not have to be fools.

Suppose he was your husband once, and that he beat you or betrayed you until you just could not put up with it anymore and you left him. Now to heal yourself, you are ready to forgive him, ready to clean the garbage of spite and resentment out of your life.

But suppose he has given you reason to believe that if you went back to him, he would soon be back at his old abuse again. Don't go back to him. Forgive him and pray that he will be changed. But don't go back. Remember: You may be a forgiver, but forgivers do not have to be fools.

PRAY: *Ask God to help you and those you love exercise wisdom and discernment in the process of becoming forgivers.*

Happiness in God's Hands

For I will forgive their wickedness and will remember their sins no more.

HEBREWS 8:12

Some people believe that you should not forgive anyone who wronged you unless he or she crawls back on his knees, says he or she is sorry, and begs your forgiveness. I think that is a bad idea.

If you wait for the lout who hurt you to repent, you may have to wait forever. And then you are the one who is stuck with the pain. If you wait for the person who hurt you to say she's sorry, you are giving her permission to keep on hurting you as long as you live.

Why should you put your future happiness in the hands of an unrepentant person who had hurt you so unfairly to begin with? If you refuse to forgive until he begs you to forgive, you are letting him decide for you when you may be healed of the memory of the rotten thing he did to you.

Why put your happiness in the hands of the person who made you unhappy in the first place? Forgive and let the other person do what he wants. Heal yourself.

REFLECT: *In whose hands are you putting your present and future happiness?*

Be Patient with Yourself

Be completely humble and gentle; be patient, bearing with one another in love.

EPHESIANS 4:2

Some people suppose that you should be able to forgive everything in a single minute and be done with it. I think they are very wrong. God can forgive in the twinkling of an eye, but we are not God. Most of us need some time. Especially if the hurt went deep and the wrong was bad. So when you forgive, be patient with yourself.

When you decide to forgive, you first make a baby step on the way to healing. And then you go on from there. You may be on the way for a long time before you finish the job. And you may backslide and need to forgive all over again.

Nobody but God is a real pro at forgiving. We are amateurs and bunglers. We cannot usually finish it the first time. So be patient with yourself. Make the first step. It will get you going, and once on the way, you will never want to go back.

JOURNAL: *As you consider your journeys in forgiveness, at its best what has your process been like? What do you hope to do differently in the future?*

Five Points on Forgiveness

Forgive us our debts, as we also have forgiven our debtors.

MATTHEW 6:12

These are the five things I want to tell you about forgiving somebody who wronged you:

1. Forgiving is the only way to be fair to yourself after someone hurts you unfairly.

2. Forgivers are not doormats; they do not have to tolerate the bad things that they forgive.

3. Forgivers are not fools; they forgive and heal themselves, but they do not have to go back for more abuse.

4. We don't have to wait until the other person repents before we forgive him or her and heal ourselves.

5. Forgiving is a journey. For us, it takes time, so be patient and don't get discouraged if you backslide and have to do it over again.

When you forgive a person who wronged you, you set a prisoner free, and then you discover that the prisoner you set free is you. When you forgive, you walk hand in hand with the very God who forgives you everything for the sake of his Son. When you forgive, you heal the hurts you never should have felt in the first place.

PRAY: *Pray that our Lord will grant you the grace of remembering these five steps for effectiveness in that journey, today and in the future.*

MONDAY *Behind the Eyes*

> *Forgive . . . from your heart.*
>
> MATTHEW 18:35

I have heard that 80 percent of what we see lies behind our eyes. If this is so, 80 percent of what we see when we look at a person who recently wronged and deeply wounded us must lie behind our eyes in the memory of our pain. We filter the image of our villain through the gauze of our wounded memories, and in the process we alter his reality.

We shrink him to the size of what he did to us; he *becomes* the wrong he did. If he has done something truly horrible, we say things like, "He is no more than an animal." Or, "He is nothing but a cheat." Our "no more thans" and our "nothing buts" knock the humanity out of our enemy. He is no longer a fragile spirit living on the fringes of extinction. He is no longer a confusing mixture of good and evil. He is only, he is totally, the sinner who did us wrong.

PRAY: *Ask God to help you keep the humanity of all people—the confusing mixture of good and bad—in your sights at all times.*

Vengeance and Justice

> *Do not seek revenge or bear a grudge against one of your people,*
> *but love your neighbor as yourself. I am the LORD.*
>
> L E V I T I C U S   1 9 : 1 8

As we move along a step or two on the path of forgiving, we hold the right to vengeance in our two hands, take one last longing look at it and let it spill to the ground like a handful of water. With good riddance.

But take care. When you give up vengeance, make sure you are not giving up on justice. The line between the two is faint, unsteady and fine. What is the difference between the two? Vengeance is our own pleasure of seeing someone who hurt us getting it back and then some. Justice, on the other hand, is secured when someone pays a fair penalty for wronging another even if the injured person takes no pleasure in the transaction. Vengeance is personal satisfaction. Justice is moral accounting.

R E F L E C T : *Do the distinctions between vengeance and justice make sense to you? Would you add any other differences? Why is justice the better way for the follower of Christ?*

Close to Justice

> *The LORD is slow to anger, abounding in love and forgiving sin and rebellion.*
> *Yet he does not leave the guilty unpunished;*
> *he punishes the children for the sin of the fathers to the third and fourth generation.*

NUMBERS 14:18

Forgiving surrenders the right to vengeance, it never surrenders claims of justice. Therein lies a key distinction. After Pope John Paul II forgave a man who took a shot at him, a journalist commented: "One forgives in one's heart, in the sight of God, as the pope did, but the criminal still serves his time in Caesar's jail." Very true. Human forgiveness does not do away with human justice. Nor divine justice. Consider the Bible's book of Numbers: "The Lord is slow to anger . . . forgiving iniquity and transgression, but by no means clearing the guilty."

We sometimes get close to justice. We never bring closure to vengeance. In the exchange of pain the accounts are never balanced. The reason is simple. When I am on the receiving end, the pain you cause me always feels worse to me than the pain I cause you. When I am on the giving end, the pain I cause you never feels as bad to me as the pain you cause me. This is why famous family feuds go on to the third and fourth generation. Vengeance by its nature cannot bring resolution.

PRAY: *Ask God to keep you from trying to balance accounts in the exchange of pain, and to seek justice—not vengeance—as a characteristic of your life.*

God's Own Art

Through Jesus the forgiveness of sins is proclaimed to you.

ACTS 13:38

Forgiving is not meant for every pain people cause us. Never has been, anymore than Prozac was invented to cure the Monday morning blahs. Forgiving is for the wounds that stab at our souls, for wrongs that we cannot put up with, ever, from anyone. When we forgive people for things that do not need forgiving we dilute the power, spoil the beauty and interrupt the healing of forgiveness. But when we forgive the things forgiving is for, we copy God's own art.

God is the original, master forgiver. Each time we grope our reluctant way through the minor miracle of forgiving, we are imitating his style. I am not at all sure that any of us would have had imagination enough to see the possibilities in this way to heal the wrongs of this life had he not done it first.

JOURNAL: *Using a Bible tool such as biblegateway.com or the* NIV Exhaustive Concordance, *do a word search on the word* forgiveness. *Write down the examples you find of God's work as the original, master forgiver. What are the elements of "God's own art" of forgiving? How can you imitate that art?*

A Genuine Repentance

Produce fruit in keeping with repentance.

MATTHEW 3:8

Desmond Tutu, spiritual leader for many in South Africa, answered for the wounded and the wronged of his beloved country. He gave his answer in a straightforward speech that bears the title "We Forgive You" (published in a collection of Tutu's speeches under the title *The Rainbow People of God,* 1994). Forgive, yes, said Tutu: "The victims of injustice and oppression must be ever ready to forgive." But could there ever be a coming together?

Ah, that is another question. "Those who have wronged (us) must be ready to make what amends they can. . . . If I have stolen your pen, I can't really be contrite when I say, 'Please forgive me' if at the same time I still keep your pen. If I am truly repentant, then I will demonstrate this genuine repentance by returning your pen. Then (reunion), which is always costly, will happen. . . . It can't happen just by saying, 'Let bygones be bygones.'"

We can forgive him if he keeps the pen. We should not be his friend unless he gives it back.

REFLECT: *What allows people like Desmond Tutu and Nelson Mandela to forgive their oppressors, or Pope John Paul II to forgive the man who attempted to kill him—rather than seek retribution? Is this a sign of strength or of weakness in their lives? Why?*

Embracing Reconciliation

> *God was reconciling the world to himself in Christ. . . .*
> *And he has committed to us the message of reconciliation.*

2 CORINTHIANS 5:19

Forgiving is completed in the mind of the person who forgives. When we forgive, we see the person who wounded us as a fellow human being worthy of our love, and in that sense we reconcile ourselves to him.

But being reconciled to him as a human being and embracing him as a partner are two different things, and we should keep them apart. If we have forgiven, we have removed one obstacle to reunion—the wall of our own bitterness. Whether we heal the relationship depends pretty much on the forgiven person.

PRAY: *If there are relationships in your life that still need a measure of reconciliation, pray for the ability of both parties to remove "obstacles to reunion" and bring healing.*

M O N D A Y

No Substitute for Prudence

If someone is caught in a sin, you who are spiritual should restore him gently.
But watch yourself, or you also may be tempted.

GALATIANS 6:1

In the warm glow of forgiving, we may want to use forgiving as a substitute for prudence and justice. But they belong in different categories.

Forgiving is a personal experience that happens inside one person at a time. What happens to the other person, the one we forgive, is up to him. And whether we restore him to the job or the place in society he had before he betrayed us and before we forgave him depends on reasonable judgments about justice and public safety. If we keep all these things—forgiving and judgment and good sense—in their right places, we can let the miracle of forgiving do its own proper work of healing and leave the restoration of the offender to other practical considerations.

PRAY: *Ask God to help you keep forgiving, with judgment and good sense in their proper places so "the miracle of forgiving" can do its proper work in your life.*

A Forgiver's Qualification

If an enemy were insulting me, I could endure it; . . .
But it is you, a man like myself, my companion, my close friend.

PSALM 55:12-13

Discerning people have an eye for moral differences. When someone hurts them accidentally, they accept it as one of the risks of living around clumsy people. But when they realize that it was no accident, they know that they were not only wounded, they were wronged besides. This is the kind of moral discernment that qualifies a person for forgiving.

We are wronged if a friend betrays our secrets, or a parent abuses us, or a partner steals from us, or a colleague lies about us and costs us a promotion. We are wronged whenever someone uses our trust to exploit us.

Of course, anybody can be wrong about being wronged. We can be conspirators in our own suffering; we may actually have encouraged the person to take advantage of us. Or we may think the other person meant to injure us when in fact we have been victims of a sheer accident. And if it comes down to it, we may have deserved what he or she did to us. We may *feel* wronged when in fact we are only wounded.

REFLECT: *How do you respond to the accidental wrongs that are part of the risks of "living around clumsy people"? How can we develop a discerning eye to know the difference between this and when we are truly wronged?*

An Overspending Grace

I am your servant; give me discernment that I may understand your statutes.

PSALM 119:125

None of us forgives with 20/20 vision. I suppose that many of us have forgiven somebody who did not really need to be forgiven. And it is probably better to forgive too much than to forgive too little. Grace can afford a bit of overspending.

Still the rule holds: To qualify as a forgiver, one needs the discernment to know that what she suffered, she suffered unfairly, that she has not just been hurt but offended and wronged as well.

PRAY: *Offer thanks to God for his "overspending" grace. Invite him to help you forgive too much, rather than too little.*

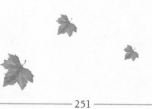

Who Can Forgive?

All the people, . . . when they heard Jesus' words,
acknowledged that God's way was right.

LUKE 7:29

Some of my Christian friends wonder whether "unbelievers" have the inner push needed to forgive someone who stung them badly. I understand their question. Forgiving is the key to the entire Christian agenda. Christ himself said that if we don't forgive people for what they do to us, we cannot expect God to forgive us for what we do to him. And did he not himself forgive just about every sorry sinner who came his way, on the spot, no questions asked? Christians certainly have strong motives for trying harder. But does this mean that only Christians can forgive?

I do not think so. I have now and then known people who did not share my faith but who acted the way I should act if I were a better Christian. They seem to be better at forgiving than I am.

So I choose not to worry about whether other people are less qualified to forgive than I am. It is hard enough for me to do it. Why should I bother my head about whether others can do it as well as I can?

REFLECT: *Who are some non-Christian role models of forgiveness? How can their example help you practice forgiveness more consistently?*

Roots of Redeeming Graces

In him we have redemption through his blood, the forgiveness of sins,
in accordance with the riches of God's grace.

EPHESIANS 1:7

We forgive when we feel a strong wish to be free from the pain that glues us to a bruised moment of the past. We forgive when we want to overcome the resentment that separates us from the person who wounded us. We forgive when we feel God's Spirit nudging us with an impulse to pull ourselves out of the sludge of our disabling resentment. We forgive when we are ready to move toward a future unshackled from a painful past we cannot undo.

Where does the desire to forgive come from? I believe that every ordinary human desire to redeem the past comes from God, the source of all redeeming graces. So one way to get the desire is to be in touch with God. The hitch is that if we do not want it, we are not likely to ask for it. But we are double-minded creatures. We all know what it is like to ferociously want something at one level and fearfully not want it at another level. And the odd thing is that sometimes the more we want something, the more we abhor the thought of having it. It is often this way with forgiving.

PRAY: *Offer thanks to God for being the source of all redeeming graces, including the desire to forgive and be forgiven.*

A Bitter Taste

> *When you stand praying, if you hold anything against anyone, forgive him,*
> *so that your Father in heaven may forgive you your sins.*

MARK 11:25

When we get obsessed with what someone did to us, when we cannot get it out of our minds night or day, when our rage churns to a froth, and, in short, when we feel most miserable, we swear that we would not forgive someone if he came crawling on his belly. But as we discover that the resentment that tasted sweet for breakfast is bitter fare for dinner, we begin to wonder whether we shall ever be happy again. And we begin to feel a wisp of a desire to get rid of the sour aftertaste of hate.

It is at this precious moment when we begin to think that perhaps we really do, after all, want healing, that we should quickly pray for more of the desire that has already begun to nudge us. Once we begin to pray, our prayer may stimulate our desire for what we pray for. And God will give that desire a shove.

PRAY: *Ask God to nurture in you a greater desire for wholeness and healing from the sour aftertaste of resentment.*

MONDAY *Unbalanced Scales*

Do not take revenge, my friends, but leave room for God's wrath, for it is written:
"It is mine to avenge; I will repay," says the Lord.

ROMANS 12:19

Vengeance is the only alternative to forgiving. It is, simply put, a passion to get even. We have been unfairly hurt. Life is out of whack. The scales are unbalanced. The only way to balance them and get life back to normal is to inflict as much pain on our abuser as he inflicted on us. An eye for an eye, wound for wound, insult for insult. Revenge—the ancient formula for undying futility.

The reason we cannot get even is that the victim and the victimizer never weigh pain on the same scale. One of us is always behind in the exchange of pain. If we have to get even, we are doomed to exchange wound for wound, blood for blood, pain for pain forever. Perpetual pain. Perpetual unfairness.

PRAY: *Give thanks to our God for being in charge of balancing the scales and offering, in the life of Jesus, a better way than vengeance, a better way than eye for an eye—a way of grace.*

The Quality of Our Lives

If you do what is right, will you not be accepted? But if you do not do what is right,
sin is crouching at your door; it desires to have you, but you must master it.

GENESIS 4:7

I believe that we sometimes—not always, but sometimes—do the right thing even if we know that it will cost us a lot of pain. We do what is right simply because we believe it is right. You can even say that the quality of our lives is measured by our willingness to do the right thing—even when we know it will make us pay dearly.

On the other hand, some things are just not meant to be done simply because it is our duty to do them. Some things are meant to be done only because we want to do them. Some can be done for no other reason. If we are not led to do them by our own inner impulses, they won't get done at all. Or at least they will not get done well. Forgiving is one of those things.

JOURNAL: *Think of a time when you did something that you knew had to be done—perhaps an ethical decision at work, or a confrontation with a spouse or friend. How did those decisions turn out? What was the impact of your decision on the quality of your life?*

A Better Way

> *Joseph said to them, "Don't be afraid. Am I in the place of God? . . .*
> *I will provide for you and your children." And he reassured them and spoke kindly to them.*

I think that when God says we ought to forgive, he intends something like this: "I have discovered a better way to deal with your memory of wrongful pain. It is an opportunity to do yourself a world of good. It will also put you in shape to do some good for the clod who hurt you and for a lot of other people besides. I call it forgiving. You really *ought* to try it."

The alternative to forgiving—getting even—only makes the pain last longer and feel worse. Even if we cause our enemy the worst pain we can think of, we don't feel any better for it. A sip of sweet revenge, maybe, but with no lasting joy in it. So forgiving is an opportunity to do something beneficial for ourselves and for other people in the bargain.

R E F L E C T : *How have you found forgiving others to be an "opportunity to do yourself a world of good"? What makes it a better way than sipping sweet revenge?*

Being Other~Centered

Create in me a pure heart, O God, and renew a steadfast spirit within me.
Do not cast me from your presence or take your Holy Spirit from me.
Restore to me the joy of your salvation and grant me a willing spirit, to sustain me.

PSALM 51:10-12

When we forgive someone, we give her back the humanity that is ever so worth loving. When we forgive someone, we give up on the sweet revenge we had such undeniable right to enjoy. And when we forgive, we feel like a person who has just done himself a splendid favor.

Forgiving, like loving, gives us no choice between being self-centered and other-centered. If I love someone only for my sake, my love becomes sick, uncreative, manipulative. If I love someone only for his or her sake, my love becomes fawning charity, demeaning pity. It is the same way with forgiving. We simply have no choice between self-centered forgiving and other-centered forgiving. I can do you good by forgiving you only if I do myself good by forgiving you. It is life's most happy vicious circle.

PRAY: *Reread Psalm 51:10-12 as a prayer. Thank God for the joy of your salvation in Jesus Christ.*

A No-Lose Opportunity

Who can say, "I have kept my heart pure; I am clean and without sin"?

PROVERBS 20:9

If someone comes on his knees, eyes red from weeping, heart in hand, groaning to all that he is the lowest of louses, and running over with promises never to do it again, it is easier to forgive him than if he struts in like a peacock. Forgiving the hardheaded, dry-eyed, unrepentant is hard indeed. And yet, when we realize that forgiving is the only remedy for the pain the offender left us with, the only way to heal the hurt he caused, we have an incentive to forgive no matter if his heart is hard as flint. In short, forgiving unrepentant people is a no-lose opportunity—difficult to do but with a harvest of healing.

JOURNAL: *What difficult person have you refused to forgive? Journal your feelings about this situation and person; then resolve to begin forgiving today.*

Freedom from Judgment

The sacrifices of God are a broken spirit;
a broken and contrite heart, O God, you will not despise.

PSALM 51:17

When a person asks us to forgive him, he is also asking permission to forgive himself. What he wants is more than freedom from our judgment. He wants freedom from *his own*. In one sense, we are the only ones on earth who can set him free to free himself.

We must pay for the license to forgive ourselves. We pay in the currency of remorse. Just as none but the contrite has a right to expect forgiveness from others, none but the contrite has a right to forgive himself. Remorse is a price we pay to forgive ourselves. For when we forgive ourselves, we are the forgiven as well as the forgiver.

REFLECT: *When you have asked for the forgiveness of another person, in what ways have you also been aware of finding the freedom to forgive yourself? Consider journaling your thoughts on these experiences, and what they have taught you.*

MONDAY *Exiled from Ourselves*

> *Let us draw near to God with a sincere heart in full assurance of faith,*
> *having our hearts sprinkled to cleanse us from a guilty conscience*
> *and having our bodies washed with pure water.*

HEBREWS 10:22

We feel a need to forgive ourselves because the part of us that gets blamed feels split off from the part that does the blaming. One self feels despised and rejected by the other. We are exiled from our own selves, which is no way to live. This is why we need to forgive ourselves and why it makes sense to do it: We are ripped apart inside, and forgiving ourselves is the only way we heal the split.

REFLECT: *What failing are you still unable to forgive yourself for? Ask God to help you accept his grace.*

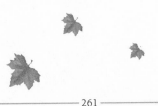

A Repeat Forgiveness

"Has not my hand made all these things,
and so they came into being?" declares the LORD.
"This is the one I esteem: he who is humble and contrite in spirit,
and trembles at my word."

ISAIAH 66:2

Self-forgiveness is not self-induced amnesia. When the memory of the horrid thing we did clicks on, the toxin of guilt spills through and condemns us again. So we need to stand before the mirror and say it again. Forgiving is seldom done once and for all. It almost always needs repeating. So say it a hundred times if you need to; say it until the meaning begins to filter through your left brain into your soul. Once you get the hang of it, the repeats will get easier and the relief will get faster.

REFLECT: *How much God must love you that he let Jesus be crucified for your sins! How important it is, then, that you accept this sacrifice and forgive yourself!*

Grace That Covers Sin

I, even I, am he who blots out your transgressions,
for my own sake, and remembers your sins no more.

ISAIAH 43:25

God covers up our sin the way a woman applies makeup over an ugly scar—so that she can look at her beauty without being put off by the blemish. Or he bends over and picks the bad thing off our backs, carries it over to the ocean, and throws it away so he won't see us with sin on our backs. Out of sight, out of mind. Then again, he washes the dirt off our faces so that he can see us for what we *are* beneath the bad things we have *done*.

In the gospel, God covers our sin with the blood that Jesus shed on the cross so he won't see our sin. Then again, he washes us with the blood of the Lamb so that he can see the real us beneath our stains and can focus on the persons he made us and is remaking us to be. In short, he covers up the wrong we *did* so that he can rediscover the persons we *are*.

JOURNAL: *Write a list of your sins today or for the week. Confess them to God, and ask his forgiveness. Then, burn the list or tear it in pieces. Let it be an image to you of God's grace.*

The Right Moment to Forgive

In him we have redemption through his blood, the forgiveness of sins,
in accordance with the riches of God's grace.

EPHESIANS 1:7

There is a right moment to forgive. We cannot predict it in advance; we can only get ourselves ready for it when it arrives. I have no more precise directions for picking the right time than this unscientific advice: Don't do it too quickly, but don't wait too long. How fast is too fast? How slow is too slow? Nobody can tell us ahead of time. Only the hurting person can know for sure when the time has come. The wise will act when it has.

APPLY: *Identify someone you've struggled to forgive. Begin to journal daily about your journey toward forgiveness of that person. Continue until you realize you've forgiven the person; take up the practice again when those feelings flare up again.*

Seventy Times Seven

> *Yet he was merciful; he forgave their iniquities and did not destroy them.*
> *Time after time he restrained his anger and did not stir up his full wrath.*

PSALM 78:38

You may have more than ample capacity to accommodate the daffiness of people you have to live with. But you also know that there is a limit. At some point, good humor ends and putting down of feet begins. So you tell him that his piddling irritations give you serious pain and that you want him to stop it.

What Jesus said about forgiving seventy times seven had nothing to do with putting up with things until the seventy times eighth offense. He was telling us not to make forgiving a matter of numbers. He was talking about healing our memories of a wound that someone's wrong etched in our cemented past. Once we have stopped the abuse, we can forgive however many times that it may take us to finish our healing.

REFLECT: *Is there any ongoing abuse you're suffering that you need to stop before you can practice forgiveness? What can you do to bring the abuse to an end?*

A Second Coat of Forgiveness

All the prophets testify about him that everyone who believes in him
receives forgiveness of sins through his name.

ACTS 10:43

There is a line in a hymn they used to sing in the hill country that celebrates the way divine forgiving closes the books on all charges against it.

The old account was settled long ago, long ago,
Long ago, long ago,
Praise God, the old account was settled long ago.

Good for God. He can forgive and be done with it. That is reassuring to know. But ordinary people are not always able to settle accounts once for all the way he does. True enough, some people manage to finish off forgiving in one swoop of the heart. But when they do, you can bet they are forgiving flesh wounds. Deeper cuts take more time and can use a second coat.

PRAY: *Pray that God will help you today to move toward forgiveness for some of the deeper cuts you've experienced.*

M O N D A Y

A Difficult Job

A man's wisdom gives him patience; it is to his glory to overlook an offense.

PROVERBS 19:11

Religious people, more than others maybe, expect to complete the project of forgiveness quickly, particularly after they have asked God to help them. With his help, they think, they should get it done on the spot and perfectly at last. What they forget is that God himself tends to baffle us with his patience about things we want done now. He is, for instance, taking his own sweet time getting the world to work right. Why should we be surprised, then, that creatures of time like us should need some time to do the difficult job of healing our wounded memories?

APPLY: *Write the name of the person you need to forgive on a Post-it note. (You may wish to use a "code" name). Put this post-it note on your refrigerator as a reminder to ask God to help you forgive him or her.*

Love's Good Servant

> *You have heard that it was said, "Love your neighbor and hate your enemy."*
> *But I tell you: Love your enemies and pray for those who persecute you.*

MATTHEW 5:43-44

The enemy of forgiving is hate, not anger. Anger is aimed at what persons do. Hate is aimed at persons. Anger keeps bad things from happening again to you. Hate wants bad things to happen to him. Anger is the positive power that pushes us toward justice. Hate, by that token, is the negative force that pushes us toward vengeance. Anger is one of love's good servants. Hate serves nobody well. So if you get angry when you remember what he or she did to you, it does not mean that you have not forgiven him. It only means that you get mad when people do bad things to you.

JOURNAL: *Journal your word associations with the words* hate *and* anger. *What do your associations tell you about your view of both? In what ways have you found anger to be "one of love's good servants"?*

A Light in Darkness

You are my lamp, O LORD; the LORD turns my darkness into light.

2 SAMUEL 22:29

Forgiving is the only way to heal the wounds of a past we cannot change and cannot forget. Forgiving changes a bitter memory into a grateful memory, a cowardly memory into a courageous memory, an enslaved memory into a free memory. Forgiving restores a self-respect that someone killed. And, more than anything else, forgiving gives birth to hope for the future after our past illusions have been shattered.

When we forgive, we bring in light where there was darkness. We summon positives to replace negatives. We open the door to an unseen future that our painful past had shut. When we forgive, we take God's hand, walk through the door and stroll into the possibilities that wait for us to make them real.

PRAY: *Confess to God your desire to forgive someone who has wronged you; ask for God's help in healing your past.*

A Way of Respect

> *Show proper respect to everyone:*
> *Love the brotherhood of believers, fear God.*

1 PETER 2:17

Morality is all about how we treat people, including ourselves. Treating people unfairly and unlovingly—this is what moral wrong is. Treating people fairly and lovingly—this is what moral right is.

Morality is about doing things to people that result in their rights being respected and their needs being tended to. It is not about living up to customs and traditions. It is not about fitting into society's traditional values. Morality is only about living in a way that respects people's rights and cares for people's needs.

This tells us what's good about being right. Being morally right is good for people. Or, to put it in reverse, being good for people is what being morally right is all about. And hurting people needlessly is what being morally wrong is all about.

REFLECT: *What have you done recently that was "morally right?" What have you done that was "morally wrong?" Take a few minutes to meditate on how you learn from both situations.*

A Confused Morality

Seek first his kingdom and his righteousness,
and all these things will be given to you as well.

MATTHEW 6:33

I know people who feel guilty whenever they displease someone, especially someone important to them. They may spend their entire lives trying to please their mothers, for example, and even when Mother is dead and gone, they still feel guilty whenever they do something that would have made her feel badly. They confuse morality with pleasing people, and the confusion leaves them feeling guilty when they may be as innocent as a baby chick.

We need to say the same thing about doing the right thing; being in the right morally is not the same as making people feel comfortable. A con artist can charm us into sweet comfort for a while, but when we discover we've been cheated, we know for sure that being a charmer is not the same as being moral.

JOURNAL: *Whose approval do you covet? Make a list. Then, journal about the difference between pleasing people and being morally right.*

Let Us Reason Together

Because I consider all your precepts right, I hate every wrong path.

PSALM 119:128

We disagree about right and wrong, of course, and why not, since we have at one time or other disagreed about almost everything else. Terrorists may believe they are doing right when they hijack an airplane and kill passengers in cold blood. You may believe they are doing a terrible wrong against humanity. So you and the terrorists disagree. Does the fact that you and the terrorists do not see eye to eye mean that neither of you can be correct?

Come now, let us reason together: Do we live in a world where nobody is ever really right or really wrong?

I don't think so. In fact, the worst thing we can do for the human family, in my opinion, is to leave right and wrong up to everybody's sovereign gut feelings.

PRAY: *Ask our Lord to help you know the difference between what is right and what is wrong, and to give you courage to speak out when something is unjust.*

MONDAY *Life's Moral Factor*

> *God created man in his own image, in the image of God he created him;*
> *male and female he created them.*

GENESIS 1:27-28

Don't we sense the moral factor in life, when it comes down to it, the way we sense that a solid rock we stubbed our toe on is real and not an illusion? For most of us, it is an intuition we could not deny if we wanted to. We cannot wash it out of our souls anymore than the ocean can wash away its own abysmal bottom; it is as natural to us as it is natural to hear the sound of music or to capture the image of sunset at sea. We see morality in life simply because our humanity is in touch with a deep design for how human beings are meant to treat each other.

APPLY: *Walk outside tonight (or on a clear night) and spend some time observing the night sky and its constellations. If God had such an amazing design for the universe, how can we doubt his design for humanity?*

A Time for Everything

There is a time for everything, and a season for every activity under heaven.

ECCLESIASTES 3:1

There is a time to sing and dance, to love and wonder, to play and work, touch our bodies and feel the wind only for the sheer joy of it. A time definitely not to give a passing thought to the right and wrong of things.

If we are not morally serious at all, we eventually turn the human family into a rat pack. But if we are morally serious about everything, we transpose the song of life too soon into a sorrow-shot dirge.

APPLY: *Plan to watch a funny movie with a friend, and let yourself experience the healing power of laughter.*

A Gracious Way

> To fear the LORD is to hate evil;
> I hate pride and arrogance, evil behavior and perverse speech.

PROVERBS 8:13

Forgiving someone is a gracious way to cope with personal pain in a world where people hurt each other unfairly. When we forgive, we transcend the pain we feel by surrendering our right to get even with the person who hurt us.

But there is a judgmental side to forgiving: No one ever forgives a person without blaming him first.

If you betray me by telling someone the secret I trusted you with—telling it, in fact, to someone who may use it against me—I will judge what you did as wrong before I ever get around to forgiving you for it. The equation goes like this: If we do not judge something to be wrong, we do not need to forgive the person who did it.

Thus, we make two judgments whenever we forgive people: we believe they did something unfair to us, and we hold them personally responsible.

REFLECT: *Who have you incompletely forgiven recently—offering forgiveness without passing judgment on their action? Ask God to help you more fully forgive in the future.*

A Moral Excellence

> *You, O Lord, are loving.*
> *Surely you will reward each person according to what he has done.*

PSALM 62:12

Think of Mother Teresa tenderly holding the head of a dying outcaste in Calcutta.

But think of yourself, too, at any moment in your life when you did something for someone, did it with no hope of a payoff, did it at some cost, did it only because that person needed you.

Think of such things and you will not need a definition of moral excellence to know it when you see it.

Now and then we make moral judgments not to decide whether we are permitted to do the sorts of things we are doing; sometimes we simply see moral goodness and we praise it, we see moral excellence and we celebrate it.

JOURNAL: *Write for five minutes, recalling a situation in which you did something for someone with no hope of a payoff and at a cost to yourself. Then write about a time when someone did this for you. Thank God for both!*

Our Pictures of Reality

There are different kinds of working, but the same God works all of them.

1 CORINTHIANS 12:6

Each of us sets the facts of his or her own picture of reality. The data speak different languages to different people. So when I say that the first job in morality is to know the facts, I am not making life easier for us.

We all filter our most significant facts through our personal beliefs, our feelings, our fears, our desires and our values. And it is only after we filter our facts that we identify them as "the facts of the case." But by this time we have given each of them a subtle new shape, and we have given each of them the meaning we believe it has. The brute facts have become personalized facts.

Nobody has exactly the same set of beliefs and values inside his or her heart that anyone else has. So the filtered facts take on as many colors and shapes as there are people who look at them.

APPLY: *Find a kaleidoscope and look through it while turning the cylinder. There are always the same pieces of colored fragments inside, but they form different designs, depending on how the cylinder is turned. In what ways is our own picture of reality similar to this? In what ways is it dissimilar?*

Who Casts the First Stone?

If any one of you is without sin, let him be the first to throw a stone.

JOHN 8:7

Once Jesus came upon some men ready to execute a woman who had been caught in an act of adultery. As far as we know, in those times a male was never taken in for adultery and certainly was never executed for it. Married men slept with other women and nobody cared very much. Married women who slept with other men became candidates for capital punishment. A man's maleness made it excusable for him to commit adultery, and a woman's femaleness made it inexcusable for her. Then Jesus came and dared any man who claimed innocence to throw the first stone. No one took his dare, and the woman went home free. The difference between him and the lynch mob was that he saw no relevant difference between male and female when it came to casting blame for adultery.

JOURNAL: *Read John 8:1-11 and rewrite the story in your own words. Reflect on Christ's mercy and grace.*

MONDAY *It Cuts Both Ways*

> *We pray to God that you will not do anything wrong.*
> *Not that people will see that we have stood the test but that*
> *you will do what is right even though we may seem to have failed.*

2 CORINTHIANS 13:7

What difference does the way we feel facts make about the rightness or wrongness of things?

It makes a lot of difference. But the difference it makes cuts two ways.

On one hand, we all need to get above our feelings about things when we make moral choices—and when we form opinions about other people's choices. We are all tempted to shunt reason to a sidetrack and let our feelings take over. The stronger we feel, the more we let our feelings substitute for thinking. If it nauseates us, we condemn it without further thought. But nausea is not morality, and feeling sick is not a ground for moral judgment.

On the other hand, if we do not feel strongly about bad things, we may be neutralized, lukewarm, indifferent. And indifferent people do not care enough to make responsible choices.

REFLECT: *How have my feelings influenced things for good? How have they influenced things badly?*

The Things That Matter Most

How much better to get wisdom than gold, to choose understanding rather than silver!

PROVERBS 16:16

We evaluate facts in terms of how important they are. Some things are more important than other things. In every human situation where somebody has to make a decision, there are gut issues and there are peripheral issues. Some factors lie at the core and matter a lot. Some factors are at the surface and do not matter much.

For a spouse, saving his or her partner's life is more important than the high cost of surgery. For an accountant, account accuracy is more important than tax savings to his or her clients. For Martin Luther King Jr., gaining justice for his people was more important than obeying segregation laws. For a corporate executive, the quality of his or her product is more important than the bottom line of this quarter's profit. When we settle on which things matter most and which matter least, we are evaluating the facts.

PRAY: *Ask our Lord to enable you to know what really matters as you evaluate facts in your decision making, and to let go of what is unimportant.*

Responsible Moral Thinking

Do not pervert justice; do not show partiality to the poor or favoritism to the great,
but judge your neighbor fairly.

LEVITICUS 19:15

The first step into responsible moral thinking is to be aware of this elementary rule: we cannot tell right from wrong unless we know the facts in the case.

We need to see them for ourselves, but we also need to know how other people see them. And we can get to know how other people see the facts only as we listen to them when they tell us what they see.

When we patiently listen to each other, and learn how the other person sees, interprets, feels, and values the facts, we discover facts are never mere facts.

People who have eyes to see and ears to hear, just as we do, see and hear the same facts as we do, but they hear a different message from the one we hear and they see a reality that is different from ours. If we really want the whole truth, we will let other people tell us why they see what we don't see and why they hear what we don't hear. If we listen to each other while we look at the facts, we may, together, get closer to reality than we could on our own.

REFLECT: *What situation or problem are you facing now that might be helped by listening to the opinions of those with whom you are in community?*

Genuine Listening

He makes them listen to correction and commands them to repent of their evil.

JOB 36:10

Never trust moral judgments to Lone Rangers.

To make right choices, we need to listen to each other as we reason together. We need to really listen, listen honestly—with a real desire to hear—listen with respect, listen with empathy, and listen with a humble sense of our own fallibility.

Be warned: genuine listening is risky. If we listen, really listen, we may adjust our own vision of the facts, we may revise our sense of their relevance, qualify our interpretation of them, modulate our feelings about them and modify our evaluation of them. But the truth about the facts is that if we look at them through our eyes alone, we may miss their meanings, and if we look at them with other people, people we respect, we have that much better chance of seeing them right—and a much better chance, too, of making good choices when we decide what to do about them.

APPLY: *Using the above as a guide, choose to listen well to the next person who disagrees with you. Then reflect on how listening affected your own views.*

Keeping Our Promises

> *Moses summoned all Israel and said: Hear, O Israel,*
> *the decrees and laws I declare in your hearing today.*
> *Learn them and be sure to follow them.*

DEUTERONOMY 5:1

When we go by the rules, we know beforehand that we should keep our promises, and that we ought not to take something that belongs to someone else. And we know a lot of other things besides.

We are like a relief pitcher in baseball who thinks ahead—before he is called into the game—and knows what pitches he should throw to each hitter in different situations; he does not have to do his thinking on the mound when he faces the league's leading hitter. Or we are like a quarterback who enters the football game with plays that he knows ahead of time are right for specific situations; he doesn't have to improvise every step along the way.

JOURNAL: *Jot down five "rules" you have learned. Reflect on how each rule has helped you in a difficult situation.*

Navigation on the Journey

In my inner being I delight in God's law.

ROMANS 7:22

Moral rules give us the same sort of help in deciding what to do in all the strange situations of modern life that a road map gives any driver trying to make his or her way along the twisting country roads of a foreign place. Our world has become a strange country to us, in many ways. And some reliable guidelines come in hand.

On the other hand, I have not yet found a set of moral rules that would relieve us of all personal responsibility for thinking and struggling and praying for wisdom in today's labyrinthian complexity.

PRAY: *Ask God to clear through confusion you may be facing and to guide you in your decision-making processes.*

MONDAY

Following Rules of Thumb

Let the wise listen and add to their learning, and let the discerning get guidance—
for understanding proverbs and parables, the sayings and riddles of the wise.

PROVERBS 1:5-6

We garner many rules from the storehouse of human wisdom. We learn by experience, and what this generation learns it passes on to the next generation in the form of proverbs, maxims and rules. Yesterday's lessons become today's wisdom. So if we follow the rules of prudence, we stand a fine chance of doing well, because the rules were distilled from the learning experience of people who came before us.

Rules of prudence tend to look like these: "Honesty is the best policy." "Women and children first." "Get a good night's sleep before you make an important decision." "Neither a lender nor a borrower be." "Never put off until tomorrow what you can do today." "Buy low, sell high." All rules of prudence.

Rules like these are "rules of thumb." All things being equal, we do well to follow them.

REFLECT: *Think of one rule you have learned by experience. Now, think of another that was passed on to you from a previous generation. Meditate on both.*

> *You must always be careful to keep the decrees and ordinances,*
> *the laws and commands he wrote for you. Do not worship other gods.*

2 KINGS 17:37

People who believe in God also believe that moral rules are God's rules. And that God's rules are also the rules of human nature. After all, if they are rules of the God who made us, they are naturally rules that fit who and what we are. We may get to know them via our conscience or via the Bible, but they come *from* God and therefore *are* the rules of human nature.

If an intelligent Creator made us, it stands to reason that he had a design for the sort of life he meant for us to live. So we should not be surprised if he furnished us with some instructions on how best to match our lives to his design. Or, in other words, how to bring out the best in our own selves.

His rules are user-friendly. Guides to humane living.

JOURNAL: *List some qualities that the rules of God would share. Spend some time reflecting on how these might help you find a "liveable morality."*

Recovering Our Moral Map

*Love the LORD your God and keep his requirements,
his decrees, his laws and his commands always.*

DEUTERONOMY 11:1

If the moral rules do in fact originate with our Creator, they are likely to have certain qualities that would be important for anyone looking for a liveable morality. If rules coming from God are at the same time the rules of human nature, we can expect them to share certain qualities.

They are not whimsical commands that a hard-driving deity throws down from heaven to make life less fun for his frolicking children. They fit what we are; if we follow them, we will function roughly the way our very nature inclines us to function. In short, what we ought to *do* matches what we are meant to *be*.

If a single set of moral rules fits all of us, we probably all share a human nature, all grow as parts of a single family tree with roots and branches stretching through all the cultures we have made and all the epochs we have survived.

Moral rules point us to where our basic inclinations lead us; moral rules are the mirrors of our most basic human tendencies.

PRAY: *Ask the Lord to bring a harmony between what you are meant to be and what you do, through the power of the Holy Spirit.*

A Rational Form

You warned them to return to your law,
but they became arrogant and disobeyed your commands.
They sinned against your ordinances, by which a man will live if he obeys them.
Stubbornly they turned their backs on you, became stiff-necked and refused to listen.

NEHEMIAH 9:29

We have all lost a lot of moral energy, just as some of us have lost our moral map. And we have followed a lot of destructive inclinations alien to our true natures. But this is a failure in the way we have handled our lives; it is not a failure in the design.

Anyone can understand God's moral manual. He does not grunt his will. Or give hand signals that only initiated members can read. His rules come to rational people in rational form.

Though not all people believe that moral rules ultimately derive from God, they can hardly misunderstand them. Take a sentence like "It is wrong to kill an innocent human being." Is this a dark and puzzling message that only insiders can decode? Does anyone have to sweat over the rule "Always keep your promises" as if it were the riddle of the Sphinx?

REFLECT: *When have you deliberately misunderstood a moral rule because it conflicted with your own desires? Confess this to God, and ask his forgiveness.*

Rules for Religion

> *I pray that out of his glorious riches he may strengthen you with power*
> *through his Spirit in your inner being, so that Christ may dwell in your hearts through faith.*
> *And I pray that you, being rooted and established in love,*
> *may have power, together with all the saints,*
> *to grasp how wide and long and high and deep is the love of Christ.*

EPHESIANS 3:16-18

It is one thing to believe that moral rules ultimately come from God. It is another thing to suppose that all rules coming from God are moral rules. God has a stake in more things than morality.

There are rules for religion, for instance.

Morality is about doing right things. Religion is about being forgiven for the wrong things we have done. The rules of morality tell us how to live well with each other. The rules of religion tell us how to live well with God.

When we say that religious rules are about our life with God and moral rules are about our life with each other, we do not mean that morality goes no deeper than human relationships. God no doubt feels very strongly about morality. Morality is rooted in God, and immorality can ruin our friendship with him. It is just that the word *morality* is the word we keep for talking about right and wrong among ourselves.

PRAY: *Thank God for his care and guidance not only for your life with him but also your life with others on earth.*

Love as Action, Not Talk

Love the Lord your God with all your heart and with all your soul and with all your strength and with all your mind. . . . Love your neighbor as yourself.

LUKE 10:27

Love and justice need each other the way our skeletons need flesh and the way our flesh needs a skeleton. We will feel the symbiosis if we recall the following ancient tale.

Jesus told a short story that has probably taught more people about real love than any story ever told. It is about a member of a minority group, a Samaritan, a salesman maybe, on a business trip to the city of Jericho. On his way he saw a man who had been mugged and left to die, bleeding in the ditch. Two other men, both of them religious teachers, had seen him too, but they were behind schedule on their divine missions, and they passed the poor fellow by. But the Samaritan stopped, personally bound the stranger's wounds, and paid a night's lodging for him at an inn before he went on; late, probably, for his appointment in Jericho. Chances are he lost a sizeable order for Judean flags.

This story illustrates that the rule of love asks us to help people, even strangers, who need us even if it costs us something, and that what love wants is *action* and not just a lot of talk.

JOURNAL: *Rewrite the story of the good Samaritan using modern-day situations and people. How does this refresh the story for you?*

MONDAY *The Rules of Strategy*

The Sabbath was made for man, not man for the Sabbath.

MARK 2:27

Jesus was taking a walk with his friends on a Sabbath afternoon and, getting a little hungry, they all picked up some whole grain from a field and enjoyed munching it while they talked. Ancient rules of strategy did not allow Jews to pick grain on the Sabbath day. So some Pharisees scolded Jesus for doing it. But Jesus did not feel bound by their rules of strategy. He was ready to change the strategy if it made for a more humane life on the Sabbath.

For Jesus, the abiding laws were all about keeping life as humane as possible. "The Sabbath was made for man," he said, "not man for the Sabbath." And rules of strategy are only devices to help us keep life as humane as we can under the circumstances. When older rules of strategy don't work well anymore, we should drop them and make new ones.

REFLECT: *What "old rules" do you need to let go of? How will you do this?*

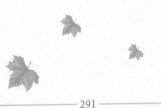

> *Obey me, and I will be your God and you will be my people.*
> *Walk in all the ways I command you, that it may go well with you.*

JEREMIAH 7:23

What are moral rules for? They are signs that point us toward a good life. This is what rules are for: they tell us how to live in ways that contribute to the goodness of human life—our own and our neighbors'.

Rules are not sacred or even good in themselves. They are means, not ends. We are obligated by the rules because we ought to live the kind of life that ends in happiness for others and for ourselves.

The point of view I have been expressing here is a version of what professionals call teleological, from *telos*, a Greek word that carries the notion of an *end* or a *goal* or a *purpose*; it is the view that morality and moral rules are really all about harmonizing our lives with the goal of the good and the happy humanity that the Creator dreamed for us.

PRAY: *Ask God to convict you when you stubbornly hold on to rules rather than caring for others, and to let you know when you have erred in being "right."*

What Matters Morally

Love does no harm to its neighbor.
Therefore love is the fulfillment of the law.

ROMANS 13:10

Justice means being fair. And how can we tell whether we have been fair to people if we do not take into account how they have been affected by what we do?

Love means being helpful. And how can we tell whether we have been helpful to people unless we know whether something good has happened to them as a result of what we did?

If you really want to be fair and if you really want to be loving to people, you have to let the results of your actions tell you whether, in real life, you are in fact being fair and loving for them.

Living right morally means living in ways that bring good things to people. And it means preventing bad things from happening to them. What really matters morally is whether we are adding to the goodness of people's lives. And for this reason alone, being moral means that we calculate the results of what we do before we can be sure that we are doing the right thing.

JOURNAL: *Think of one current situation in which your actions may change someone's life for good or for bad. Meditating on the passage above, how might you act?*

The World's Good Things

How priceless is your unfailing love!
Both high and low among men find refuge in the shadow of your wings.

PSALM 36:7

The world is filled with a fantastic, bewildering number of good things, like cows and children, stars and sonnets, families and freedom, birds and books, all sorts of things. Good things are so different from each other we wonder how in the world they can be enough alike for us to attach the adjective "good" to them all.

But while countless things are good, some things are better, in some ways, than other good things are, and one of the more splendid talents any serious person can have is the ability to sense which things are worth more and which are worth less. This will be the person who can tell what price he or she ought to pay for desired things. And, of course, when we speak of price, we are talking about more than dollars and cents.

REFLECT: *What is most valuable to you? Why?*

Experiencing God

> Well done, good and faithful servant! You have been faithful with a few things;
> I will put you in charge of many things. Come and share your master's happiness!

MATTHEW 25:21

An experience of God has several dimensions, each of which is vital to our lasting happiness. When we experience God, we experience

- the Creator who is the living source of our very being;
- the Savior who forgives all our failures;
- the Spirit who enables us to move toward wholeness, and who nudges us to hang on, by our fingernails sometimes, because we know that in the end happiness will win out over sadness and sorrow.

These are the inner sources of the happiness we feel even when other segments of life get grim.

REFLECT: *When has this inner source of happiness seen you through a difficult time? How might this experience encourage you when you encounter something difficult?*

A World of Wonders

You make me glad by your deeds, O LORD;
I sing for joy at the works of your hands.

PSALM 92:4

People sometimes talk as if they need only God in order to be happy. But the good news is that the Creator never meant us to have him only. Why else would he have made us so needy for friends and lovers? Why else would he have created us so ripe for sweet fruits and joyous sounds? Why else would he have given us eyes to look in beauty's face, ears to hear happy human voices, skin to feel the touches of affection? And why else would he have set us down in a world so filled with things we relish? He made us so that we could have all this and heaven too. Or, better, heaven, too, in the midst of all this.

APPLY: *Spend at least fifteen minutes sitting outside in a quiet place. Use your five senses to appreciate the world God has made.*

MONDAY

A Generous God

> *Our mouths were filled with laughter, our tongues with songs of joy.*
> *Then it was said among the nations, "The LORD has done great things for them."*
>
> PSALM 126:2

God is generous enough to give us himself and his splendid gifts besides.

What bearing does all this have on how we can know whether actions are right or wrong?

Just this: if what you do brings about greater happiness for people, including yourself, there is a good chance that what you are doing is right.

Remember, we are not talking about pleasure. Giving people pleasure is not at all a sign that what you are doing is right, any more than it is a sign that you are doing wrong. But whatever we do that increases people's health, assures their freedom, creates beauty out of squalor, deepens their gratitude and so on is likely to be right.

APPLY: *Think of one right action you can take that will improve the happiness of another, and be intentional about doing it today.*

Who Takes Credit?

*Surely goodness and love will follow me all the days of my life,
and I will dwell in the house of the LORD forever.*

PSALM 23:6

Morality is always about keeping life good, or making it better, or preventing it from getting worse than it already is. This is why it is good to be a good person. Not so that you get God to applaud you. But so that you do some good for your friends and neighbors, even for your enemies.

Moral virtues are not the only good qualities worth having. It is good to be charming, and smart, and assertive. It is good, too, to be talented and imaginative, with a splendid streak of self-esteem thrown in. But you are not what we would call a good person just because you are lucky enough to possess these positive powers. Fortunate, yes. Good? Not necessarily.

How much credit anyone actually deserves for being a good person is hard to say. Most of our moral qualities are gifts of God. Or hand-me-downs from good parents and a good environment. So if we do have good characters, we have more reason to give thanks than to congratulate ourselves.

PRAY: *Ask our Lord to forgive you at times when you take pride in your "goodness" and instead to direct the glory toward him.*

Not by Rules Alone

Religion that God our Father accepts as pure and faultless is this:
to look after orphans and widows in their distress
and to keep oneself from being polluted by the world.

JAMES 1:27

Results matter, and they matter a lot. It would curdle the milk of human kindness if we steered our moral lives without keeping a kindly eye on how our acts touch the lives of other people.

We cannot live by moral rules alone, not in a broken world, a crazy world where to obey one rule can compel you to break another and where being right according to the rules can be wrong according to what it does to people.

We cannot live by results alone, either, not in a complex world where results that feel good today can go sour on us later, and where good results for some people bring disaster to others.

PRAY: *Ask our Lord to increase your awareness of how your actions today will affect other people.*

Through the Freedom Zones

The creation was subjected to frustration, not by its own choice,
but by the will of the one who subjected it, in hope that the creation itself
will be liberated from its bondage to decay and brought into
the glorious freedom of the children of God.

ROMANS 8 : 2 0 - 2 1

To live a successful moral life, we need to follow the rules while we keep a sharp eye on the results of what we do. But we can shift the sentence around and it would be just as true. To live a successful moral life, we need to keep a sharp eye on the results of what we do while we follow the moral rules.

But most of the time we maneuver our ways through freedom zones where what matters is not whether we have done the right thing but whether we acted wisely and well considering the options we had. There are huge areas in our lives where the question is not whether we did right or wrong but only whether we acted like responsible people.

R E F L E C T : *Think back on a time you acted responsibly, and a time you acted ir-*
responsibly. How might you learn from both situations?

A Seasoned Discernment

> *A discerning man keeps wisdom in view,*
> *but a fool's eyes wander to the ends of the earth.*

PROVERBS 17:24

The first test of responsible action is whether we have kept our eyes and ears open to what is going on. So that we will know when to "hold 'em" and when to "fold 'em."

The name for this ability is *discernment*. We have it when we can be depended on to sense what is really going on around us and what is the better thing to do about it.

Some people always seem to notice things that other people miss; they catch little touches that are terribly important but seldom obvious to people who never look beneath the surface. They see subtle shifts in body language, hear delicate messages in other people's tones of voice, catch quiet hints that less sensitive people never notice. They have discernment.

JOURNAL: *Look up the definition of* discernment *in the dictionary. Write it in your journal, then write as many attributes of discernment that you can imagine. Choose one attribute to try and implement in your life.*

Taking Your Time

He changes times and seasons; he sets up kings and deposes them.
He gives wisdom to the wise and knowledge to the discerning.

DANIEL 2:21

Discernment separates the moral artist from the moral bungler. Bunglers know the rules but do not see what is going on in front of their eyes. They do not make good choices because they have not discerned what the situation calls for—the more helpful words, the more useful actions for *that* occasion.

If you are discerning, you take your time. You do not act until you catch an insight into what is going on in other people's feelings, into what is really on people's minds, into what people really need at the time. You wait, you check your impulse to shoot from the hip, you do nothing, say nothing, until you have gotten a good sense of what the situation really calls for.

APPLY: *Go for a short walk. As you walk, think about ways to curb your impatience, become a better listener and discern what people are telling you.*

MONDAY *A Responsible Person*

When a man makes a vow to the LORD or takes an oath to obligate himself by a pledge,
he must not break his word but must do everything he said.

NUMBERS 30:2

Responsible people dare to make and care to keep commitments. They also know when to break a commitment badly made and wrong to keep.

What do we do when we make a commitment? What sort of thing is a commitment, and why should we be bound to any we make? We make many kinds of commitments, of course—to people, to causes, to beliefs, to institutions.

When we make a commitment to someone, we promise to be with him or her at any unspecified time in the future. We make an open-ended appointment for any tomorrow. We stretch ourselves into the unpredictable future and make one thing predictable: we will be there when needed. No matter what the circumstances are.

REFLECT: *How do you feel when someone breaks a commitment to you? How can you do better keeping your own commitments?*

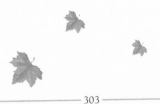

Commitments to Break

Surely you desire truth in the inner parts;
you teach me wisdom in the inmost place.

PSALM 51:6

Some commitments should never be made. And once made ought to be broken as fast as possible. Remember Albert Speer, Hitler's brilliant architect? When he came to the end of the evil road he had traveled and wondered how he could have gone so deeply into Hitler's hell, he came up with this answer: he committed himself to Hitler when he joined the Nazi youth corps and never examined his commitment again.

He could have gotten out early on, but he kept his commitment out of blind, uncritical loyalty to a madman. When Speer finally woke up, too late, and turned against Hitler, the worst accusation Hermann Göring, loyal head of Hitler's Luftwaffe, could level at him was "You broke our commitment." Alas, if he had only broken his promise two decades earlier.

REFLECT: *What wrong commitments have you made? If you have not broken them already, think about what needs to happen in order to set things right.*

Testing Our Responsibility

Do not forsake wisdom, and she will protect you;
love her, and she will watch over you.

PROVERBS 4:6

People who keep their bags packed, ready to move out of other people's lives whenever the grass looks greener down the street, leaving those they love behind to pick up the pieces, people who do not care enough to stick it out through long, cold winters with anybody or anything, are usually people who have opted for the self-centered life in which nobody is responsible for anything.

So one way to test our responsibility is to ask whether what we are doing matches up with the important commitments we have made.

JOURNAL: *Make a list of the good commitments you have made in your life. Reaffirm to God your desire to keep these commitments.*

Love's Foresight

> *Wisdom is more precious than rubies,*
> *and nothing you desire can compare with her.*

PROVERBS 8:11

In human relationships, imagination is the inward vision of love. It is love's educated guess of what will happen to another person if we do what we think is right. Imagination is compassion stretched beyond our prefabricated notions of right and wrong. Imagination is the beginning of responsible morality.

We fail to use imagination not because we were not lucky enough to inherit the gift but because we do not pull ourselves far enough above our own desires, high enough to see ahead into how what we do will touch the lives of people.

Imagination is love's foresight. Without it we are likely to act irresponsibly. So another way to make the responsibility test is to ask, "Did I stop to use imagination before I acted?"

REFLECT: *When have you been unable to rise above your own desires to think of how to touch the lives of people? How might you stretch your compassion next time?*

Loving Our Neighbor

> *Woe to those who go to great depths to hide their plans from the LORD,*
> *who do their work in darkness and think, "Who sees us? Who will know?"*

ISAIAH 29:15

We would all stay out of a lot of trouble if we always acted where people could see us. Or if we were at least willing for them to see us. Cover-ups are always the strategy of the irresponsible.

So one way of testing the responsibility of what we are doing is to ask, "Would I be willing to let people I care about know what I am doing?"

A discouraging fact about human nature is that few of us can be trusted for very long to act responsibly behind a curtain. Our yen for cover is a hint that we cannot trust ourselves totally. No wonder darkness and evil are synonymous in almost all religious myths. God is light, said the apostle John, there is no darkness in him at all. And anyone on earth who loves his neighbor is living in light.

PRAY: *Ask God to bring to your attention those things you do in secret that you know belong to darkness. Then ask his forgiveness and move forward to make changes.*

Sticking with Consequences

Better to be lowly in spirit and among the oppressed
than to share plunder with the proud.

PROVERBS 16:19

Martin Luther King Jr. had a strict rule for people who chose to follow his pilgrimage into nonviolent civil disobedience. It was this: anyone who disobeyed unjust laws had to be willing to go to jail for breaking them. You were not able to break a law and run for it, evil as the law was; the responsible way was to break the law, stay where you were and offer yourself to the police.

You had to accept the consequences of civil disobedience even in a righteous cause. If you were not willing to stay at the scene of your "crime," let everybody know what you had done and take whatever was dished out to you, you were not acting responsibly.

Sticking with the consequences was not a sure test of whether you did the right thing. But it was a fine test of whether you acted responsibly doing it.

REFLECT: *When have you made a decision in which you had to stick with the consequences? How did this affect you?*

MONDAY *Making Right Choices*

Neither height nor depth, nor anything else in all creation,
will be able to separate us from the love of God that is in Jesus Christ our Lord.

ROMANS 8:39

Morality is the need to make right choices. Forgiveness is the freedom to make wrong choices.

Dare to be wrong! Risk it! With forgiveness you discover that being wrong is not all that bad. No wrong choice you make can persuade God to love you less. Believe this and you will have new courage to make choices even when you are not sure they will be the right ones to make.

Søren Kierkegaard, the complicated Danish philosopher, once said a prayer that went something like this:

Lord, I have to make a choice, and I'm afraid that I may make the wrong one. But I have to make it anyway; and I can't put it off. So I will make it, and trust you to forgive me if I do wrong. And, Lord, I will trust you, too, to help make things right afterward.

The last word about choices is this: nothing you do wrong can get God to love you less than he did when you did things right. Nothing ever separates you from the love of God.

REFLECT: *Do you feel unworthy to be loved by God? Meditate on what it means to never be separated from his love.*

A New Creation

Jesus Christ is the same yesterday and today and forever.

HEBREWS 13:8

How can a person who lived nearly two thousand years ago radically change a human life here and now? How can Jesus of Nazareth *radically* affect us, as persons, to the depths of our being? How can he reach out over the great span of time that divides us from him and change us so profoundly that we can become "new creatures" in him?

Does the Jesus of the past become, in fact, the Jesus of the present? The apostle Paul says that he does. And this is the difference between his influence and that of any other influential person. He touches us here and now, not merely by the ripples of the historical currents he once set in motion but by entering into union with us personally. Union with Christ—this is the sum and substance of the Christian's status, the definition of his relationship to Jesus, the large reality in which all the nuances of his new being are embraced.

PRAY: *Pray that Jesus will radically affect you, your work and your relationships.*

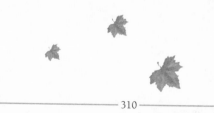

A Genuine Christian Faith

Therefore, if anyone is in Christ, he is a new creation;
the old has gone, the new has come!

2 CORINTHIANS 5:17

Paul, whose message is our primary source for the doctrine of union with Christ, talks about our being "in Christ." He also says that Christ is "in us" (Ephesians 3:17; Galatians 2:20), which would seem to be something different. Then he says that we experienced history-shaking events of the cross and resurrection along *with him*: he says that we died with Christ, were buried with Christ and were raised with Christ (Romans 6:1-4; Ephesians 2:5, 6). He drops this shocking language by the way, as it were, and inserts it into a bewildering variety of contexts, shifting the actual terminology about so that we are finally left wondering whether anyone can grasp it all.

Union with Jesus Christ is at once the center and circumference of authentic human existence. Christian faith has no genuine reality and the church no unique mission in the world if people cannot share the life and destiny of Jesus Christ.

APPLY: *Read the Scripture passages mentioned above, and think about what it means to be in union with Christ.*

The Claims of Christ

I have been crucified with Christ, and I no longer live,
but Christ lives in me.
The life I live in the body, I live by faith in the Son of God,
who loved me and gave himself for me.

GALATIANS 2:20

There is an irony in equating one's own moral insights with the mind of Christ. For in doing so one can appear humble: "This is not what *I* say, it is what Christ says," or "This is not *my* claim, it is the claim of Christ." But the disclaimer is, of course, false. For the voice and the claim are always the voice and claim of a man. And the imputation of one's own thoughts, of one's own moral judgment, to Christ is simply a subtle way of claiming absoluteness of one's self.

The life we live "in the flesh" is still the life of the proud and ignorant, the compromising and ambiguous, the devious and lustful self; this is why the life lived "in the flesh" must be a life of "faith in the Son of God." Though "Christ lives in me" is a reality, it is not a complete and total actuality. It offers a promise, but it does not undo the inner and outer contradictions of life.

JOURNAL: *How does your life today seem lived "in the flesh?" How can you turn it into a life of "faith in the Son of God?" Write some of your thoughts.*

Affirming the Faith

He was delivered over to death for our sins
and was raised to life for our justification.

ROMANS 4:25

When I affirm in faith that Christ died and rose again, I am also affirming (equally by faith) that I died and rose again, too.

When I assent to the fact that Christ died for me, I am saying that I am the kind of person who needs dying for, and was in fact died for. When I affirm that Christ rose again "for my justification," I am concurring with God's liberation of my sinful self from judgment. I do indeed "reckon myself dead to sin and live to God in Jesus Christ." And only as I affirm this in free decision and with my whole attitude and action, am I also affirming the real truth about the events that happened in past history.

PRAY: *Confess your sins before God. Ask his forgiveness. Thank him for the sacrifice that makes grace possible!*

A New Order of Life

I am the resurrection and the life. He who believes in me will live,
even though he dies; and whoever lives and believes in me will never die.

JOHN 11:25-26

If my affirmation of the facts of Jesus' death and resurrection is not one that sweeps my whole existence into its power, I am not making an affirmation of faith in the biblical sense. The statement that "Jesus died and rose again" is not in itself a statement of faith. One does not necessarily make a statement of faith when he says, "Jesus died *for me*." Both of these become statements of faith when they verbalize my entrance into the new order of life that was created when he died and rose again.

PRAY: *Give God thanks for giving his only Son, who makes us a new creation.*

MONDAY *Living in Christ*

We live by faith, not by sight.

2 CORINTHIANS 5:7

What is the relationship between the reality that we experience and our experience of that reality? The reality is union with Christ; our way of experiencing that reality is called faith. The two should be neither confused nor separated. We ought not make our faith the whole of the reality. But we must not separate them either. Faith is indispensable to union, but is not the whole of it. Yet they are interrelated in a dynamic and inseparable way.

Faith is the *how*. Union with Christ is the *what*. Faith is our way of living in Christ and with Christ, and of demonstrating the power of his living in us.

Paul has a way of mixing his references to our life of faith and our life in Christ. Paul lives "in Christ," he relates to others "in Christ," he walks and hopes "in Christ." But with the same accents he talks about living in faith. Living in Christ and living in faith come to the same thing, but only because "faith" is the multidimensional word for our whole experience of Christ.

REFLECT: *How does this reading shape the way you view faith? Meditate on what it means to have union with Christ.*

Turning Toward the Future

In keeping with his promise we are looking forward
to a new heaven and a new earth, the home of righteousness.
So then, dear friends, since you are looking forward to this,
make every effort to be found spotless, blameless and at peace with him.

2 PETER 3:13-14

Hope is faith turned toward the future. It is faith fastened in courage to the new creation which is yet to be. When in faith the Christian says, "But we anticipate a new heaven and a new earth wherein dwelleth righteousness," she is expressing faith in the form of hope. When hope is taken away, however eloquently or elegantly we discourse concerning faith, we are convicted of having none. Christian faith is life's openness to Jesus the Lord, whose Spirit is the down payment of the new creation still to come.

In the same moment that it summons us to faith, the cross summons us to hope. While it calls us to involvement in and commitment to the new creation that is present now, it also calls us to hope that the new creation will be fulfilled and visible in the future. Past, present and future converge in the decision of faith.

JOURNAL: *What does hope for the "new creation" mean to you, both in the present and the future?*

The Power of the Resurrection

He lavished on us [the riches of his grace] with all wisdom and understanding.
And he made known to us the mystery of his will according to his good pleasure,
which he purposed in Christ.

EPHESIANS 1:8-9

When we speak of faith as a form of knowing, we usually point to the content of our knowledge. *What* we know determines the way we know. What we know, in short, is this: Jesus is Lord. And the nature of this truth conditions the way we know it.

Paul says that he has "all wisdom and understanding by which the mystery of his *will* is made *known*." That revealed mystery is God's purpose to reunite a fractured world and to reconcile people to each other within it. His will is to save people who were strangers to his commonwealth. This is the mystery that is known now. To know this is to know the power of the resurrection in Christ.

PRAY: *Ask God to heal our fractured world and reconcile people to each other within it. Pray as specifically as you can.*

Knowledge of the Heart

> *My message and my preaching were not with wise and persuasive words,*
> *but with a demonstration of the Spirit's power.*

1 CORINTHIANS 2:4

How do *we* know that the last word in human history is Christ's lordship over history? There is little in history itself that will suggest it to us. It is known through the "power and the Spirit" that works through the "preaching" of Christ crucified. In short, the reality of Christ is known in the gospel preached and heard by us, and the Spirit at work within us. The reality of Christ's new order, and the firmness of our place within it, are known only as we are united to Christ himself.

But knowledge in faith is a knowledge of the heart. To know in faith is not to be theologically literate; those who know have a spirit of wisdom and revelation in the knowledge of him, having their *hearts* enlightened (Ephesians 1:17). That is, to know in faith is to know a *person* with the knowledge of the *heart*. We are talking about something more primitive and deeper than an intellectual grasp of things.

To know in faith is to know the love of Christ, which is beyond the grasp of intellect. And this requires the Spirit and the power, the presence of Christ within our hearts.

REFLECT: *What does it mean to you that the Spirit is at work in your life? Does this seem like an abstract concept? Meditate on Scriptures about the Holy Spirit, such as Luke 1:35, Luke 2:26 and John 14:26.*

A Life of Love

By faith we eagerly await through the Spirit the righteousness for which we hope.
For in Christ Jesus neither circumcision nor uncircumcision has any value.
The only thing that counts is faith expressing itself through love.

GALATIANS 5:5-6

The life in union with Christ is a life of love. And love is faith doing its work. Love is the primary form of the obedience of faith.

Paul says that faith works by love. He does not mean that love is an additive; he means that belief takes the form of love. Love *is* faith turned outward in action. Love is a fruit of the Spirit within; the acts of Christian love are impelled by the indwelling of Christ. The result of the indwelling of Christ is that love becomes the ground of our lives.

How could it be otherwise? The new creation begun at the resurrection means the reunion of people; the creation of "one new man" reconciled in Christ. The fulfillment of the new creation is the embodiment of love in life on earth.

APPLY: *Choose one way you will show love in a new or stretching way in the week to come.*

Christ as Lord

> *I believe that you are the Christ, the Son of God,*
> *who was to come into the world.*
>
> JOHN 11:27

Without persons who respond in faith, without persons who live in union with Christ, any talk about Christ as Lord would be meaningless. Christ as Lord *means* the Christ who created a new situation of which he is the representative and ruling Head, a situation so identified with him that when we are part of his situation we can be said to be "in him." Therefore, Christ is Lord only in union with those who, in faith, are committed citizens of his new creation.

But there is also no reality to faith, in the Christian sense, unless Jesus actually is Lord. The reality of faith and the reality of Christ join in the creation of our union with him. Faith is not the same as union; it is our living affirmation, in thought, in word and above all in deed, of his union with us.

JOURNAL: *What does it mean to you that Christ is Lord? How does the knowledge of this influence what you will do today?*

ABOUT THE AUTHOR

In addition to his work at Fuller Theological Seminary, Lewis B. Smedes (1921-2002) taught at Calvin College and was the author of numerous books, including the bestseller *Forgive and Forget*, as well as *Shame and Grace, Love Within Limits, A Life of Distinction, Choices* and a spiritual memoir released posthumously titled *My God and I*.

ABOUT THE EDITOR/COMPILER

Jeff Crosby is director of sales and marketing at InterVarsity Press. His writings have appeared on explorefaith.org, and in *Marriage Partnership, CBA Marketplace, Christian Retailing* and other book trade journals. He and his wife, Cindy, reside in Glen Ellyn, Illinois, and have two grown children.

THROUGH THE YEAR DEVOTIONALS

Courageous Faith
by Bill Hybels

Days of Grace
by Lewis B. Smedes

Hearing God
by Dallas Willard

Joy in the Journey
by Michael Card

Knowing God
by J. I. Packer

My Heart—Christ's Home
by Robert Boyd Munger and others